**Posters by Members of the
Alliance Graphique Internationale
1960–1985**

Edited by Rudolph de Harak

Rizzoli International Publications, Inc.
New York, New York

**Posters by Members of the
Alliance Graphique Internationale
1960–1985**

Edited by Rudolph de Harak

Rizzoli International Publications, Inc.
New York, New York

First published in the United States
of America in 1986 by
Rizzoli International Publications, Inc.
597 Fifth Avenue,
New York, NY 10017

Designed by Rudolph de Harak
Printing and binding: Dai Nippon
Printing, Japan

Library of Congress
Cataloging-in-Publication Data
Main entry under title: AGI poster book.

1. Posters–20th century. 2. Artists–
Biography. I. Alliance graphique
internationale. II. Harak, Rudolph de.
NC1806.8.A35 1986 741.67'4'0904
85-28116 ISBN 0-8478-0694-4

Table of Contents

Dedicated
to the memory of Will Burtin

Dedicated
to the memory of Will Burtin

President's statement

Poster, *affiche,* or *plakat* means "a sheet of paper," or else "to be affixed to a wall," the reference being to the object itself, nothing more. In Italian the word for poster is *manifesto,* from the verb *manifestare*—"to express or convey." To me this is the most appropriate semantic root, the one I like to think best represents the meaning of this book. This book is not about different styles or graphic modes. It is about the essence of visual expression: the poster, as the epitome of visual synthesis, the focus of visual and verbal metaphors, the place where word and image come together in perfect symbiosis.

Nothing better than the posters in this book expresses the power of design to transcend an ephemeral destination and achieve the permanence of art. These posters have been designed by some of the best designers and communications artists in this century, all members of AGI–the Alliance Graphique Internationale, the prestigious association over which I now have the honor to preside. On the occasion of the AGI conference in Montreal in 1982, a very successful exhibition of posters by AGI members was assembled which provided the core and inspiration for this book. I am sure that I represent the feelings of all AGI members in expressing to Rudy de Harak our deepest gratitude for taking the time and effort to conceive and produce this book.

AGI is coming of age, and this is one of the first books to document this extraordinary association of people who through their work have manifested the character of our age, the complexities of our social environment, and our hopes for the future. A special thanks to Gianfranco Monacelli, director of Rizzoli International Publications, New York, for his continuous support of architecture, art, and design, and for providing the documents of our time for the future.

Massimo Vignelli

Introduction

The graphic designer's work centers on visual communication, a process of problem solving that embraces aesthetics. Among the many forms this takes are books, record covers, brochures, postage stamps, billboards, corporate identity programs, and posters. But of all these, there is no richer or more exciting medium than the poster to express the creative personality of the designer.

Ever since the nineteenth century, and prior to the broad-based, sophisticated means of communication we now have at our disposal, the poster has played an important role in the social life of the community, disseminating political information and announcing cultural events. Initially its production was primarily the task of the printer. With the advent of explosive changes in all areas of art and politics, rapid development of technology in the graphic arts and printing industries, and the emergence of the profession of graphic design as we now know it, widespread experimentation was precipitated. Such artists as Alexander Rodchenko, El Lissitzky, and Piet Zwart brought to the field a new understanding of the interconnective relationship and creative possibilities of typography, photography, and rendered images, giving a dynamic vocabulary to poster design and raising the medium to a new aesthetic level.

The poster is usually found in public spaces, both indoors and outdoors. Mounted on kiosks especially designed for the purpose or affixed to walls and fences, it adds richness of color and design to a community environment. Its job is to state its message quickly and simply to an audience that is usually on the move and has little time to linger. In comparison to the magazine advertisement, it is larger in format and carries a shorter typographic message. Within these parameters it offers the designer a unique opportunity and freedom to manipulate and interrelate typography with photography and rendered form.

The posters illustrated in this book have been created by many of the most important graphic designers in the world. All are members of the Alliance Graphique Internationale, an organization formed in 1950. Its founding member-artists were Donald Brun and Fritz Bühler, both from Switzerland, and three Frenchmen—Jean Colin, Jacques Nathan-Garamond, and Jean Picart Le Doux. These five men felt there was the need for an exchange of ideas and a sharing of common interests among highly creative professional graphic designers. Membership rapidly increased to include many nationalities, climbing to just over two hundred designers practicing in twenty-four countries. Most of the members know each other well and have developed strong personal and professional relationships. A high point of AGI's activities is a congress held once a year, always in a different country. Here ideas are exchanged, members show their work, and the state of design is reviewed and debated.

The idea for this book developed at a congress held several years ago in Montreal, when AGI staged an extensive exhibition of members' posters in the public concourse of the Place Ville Marie. More than three hundred posters selected by the members themselves were displayed. The exhibition received wide press coverage and proved very popular with the people of Montreal. It reconfirmed the aesthetic value of the poster, its sense of visual excitement, its power to reach out to an audience and effectively state facts, feelings, and ideas.

Almost all of the posters in this book fall within a twenty-five-year period. Among the exceptions are two from 1929, two from the 1940s, and three from the 1950s. I felt these added richness to the book, but didn't warrant changing the title.

Rudolph de Harak

Acknowledgments

I wish to express my gratitude to the following people for their assistance:

Massimo Vignelli, president of the Alliance Graphique Internationale, the Executive Committee, and all the other members of AGI for their support and generosity in allowing their work to be published here.

Barbara Caruana of my staff for her editorial assistance and help in pulling the countless loose ends of this project together.

Todd Blank of my staff for assisting me in the design of this book, specifying type, cropping photographs, scaling transparencies, preparing mechanicals, and patiently making the many design adjustments and changes that were required.

Tom Repensek for editing and proofreading the manuscript.

Joan Ockman of Rizzoli International Publications for her advice and many constructive suggestions.

Gianfranco Monacelli, president of Rizzoli International Publications, for consenting to publish this book.

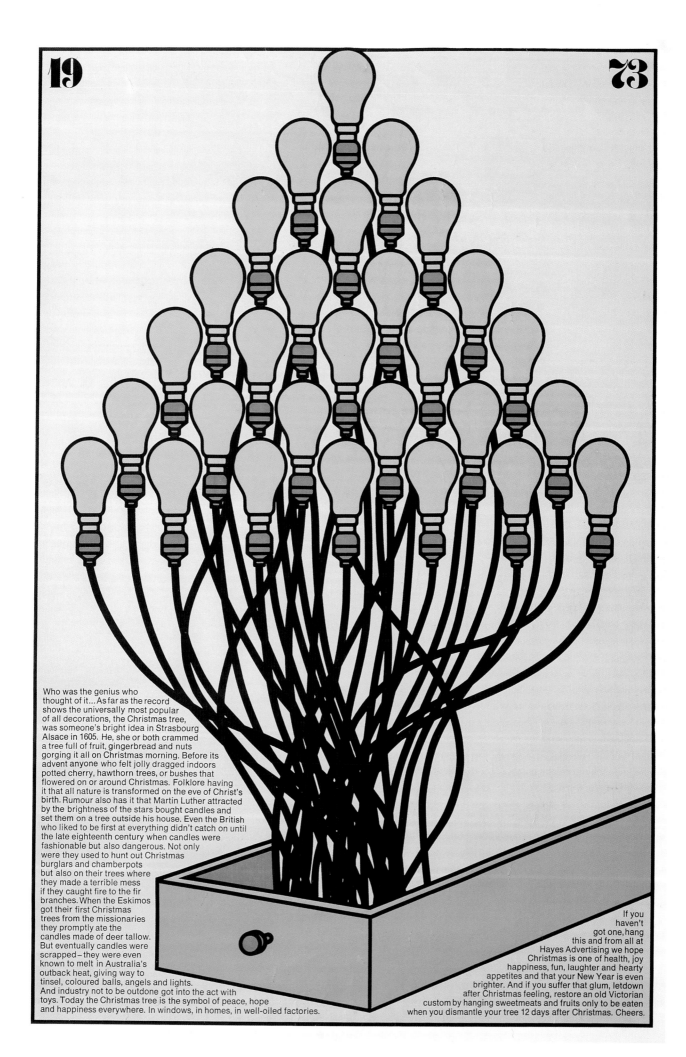

Who was the genius who thought of it... As far as the record shows the universally most popular of all decorations, the Christmas tree, was someone's bright idea in Strasbourg Alsace in 1605. He, she or both crammed a tree full of fruit, gingerbread and nuts gorging it all on Christmas morning. Before its advent anyone who felt jolly dragged indoors potted cherry, hawthorn trees, or bushes that flowered on or around Christmas. Folklore having it that all nature is transformed on the eve of Christ's birth. Rumour also has it that Martin Luther attracted by the brightness of the stars bought candles and set them on a tree outside his house. Even the British who liked to be first at everything didn't catch on until the late eighteenth century when candles were fashionable but also dangerous. Not only were they used to hunt out Christmas burglars and chamberpots but also on their trees where they made a terrible mess if they caught fire to the fir branches. When the Eskimos got their first Christmas trees from the missionaries they promptly ate the candles made of deer tallow. But eventually candles were scrapped – they were even known to melt in Australia's outback heat, giving way to tinsel, coloured balls, angels and lights. And industry not to be outdone got into the act with toys. Today the Christmas tree is the symbol of peace, hope and happiness everywhere. In windows, in homes, in well-oiled factories.

If you haven't got one, hang this and from all at Hayes Advertising we hope Christmas is one of health, joy happiness, fun, laughter and hearty appetites and that your New Year is even brighter. And if you suffer that glum, letdown after Christmas feeling, restore an old Victorian custom by hanging sweetmeats and fruits only to be eaten when you dismantle your tree 12 days after Christmas. Cheers.

CALL FOR ENTRIES. Entries Close November 21 For The Adelaide Art Directors Club 1980 Awards.

ACKNOWLEDGEMENTS: DESIGN BARRIE TUCKER & ROBERT MARSHALL. PAPER TOMASETTI. COLOUR SEPARATION B&D MODGRAPHIC. PRINTING MITCHELL PRESS.

Belgium   **Gilles Fiszman**   1980   Performance announcement
Center of Improvement and
Research for Performing Artists
20'' × 27½''

MUDRA

Centre de perfectionnement et de recherche des interprètes du spectacle
Centrum voor hogere opleiding en navorsing voor theatervertolkers
Direction générale, Maurice Béjart, Algemene directie
Directeur artistique, Micha Van Hoecke, Artistiek directeur

Gilles Fiszman

L'ATELIER RUE STE ANNE PRESENTE
TRILOGIE DU REVOIR
DE BOTHO STRAUSS

DECOR ET COSTUMES: CLAUDE LEMAIRE / MUSIQUE: JEAN-YVES BOSSEUR
REGIE GENERALE: JEAN-MARIE VERVISCH / MISE EN SCENE: PHILIPPE VAN KESSEL
AVEC HENRI BILLEN / FRANCINE BLISTIN / JEAN-CLAUDE DERUDDER / PATRICK DESCAMPS / CLAUDE ETIENNE / HÉLÈNE FRIEDLI
MICHELINE HARDY / CLAUDE KOENER / PIERRE LAROCHE / MARIE SYGNE LEDOUX / VINCENT LEMAITRE / FRANCIS MAHIEU / ESTELLE MARION
DENIS PANERAI / JEAN PASCAL / DENYSE PERIEZ / PHILIPPE PETIT / PHILIPPE VAN KESSEL
COPRODUCTION ATELIER RUE STE-ANNE / THEATRE DE LA PLACE

GRANDE SALLE / 75 RUE DES TANNEURS / 1000 BRUXELLES
DU 15 NOV. AU 15 DEC. 1984 / TOUS LES SOIRS A 20 h 15 / RELACHE DIMANCHES, LUNDIS
ET LE 5 DEC. / RESERVATIONS DE 14 A 18 h AU 02/513 19 28

AVEC L'AIDE DE LA FONDATION THEATRE ET CULTURE ET DE LA COMMUNAUTE FRANÇAISE DE BELGIQUE

Galileo

The Theatre Company at
the St. Lawrence Centre
Front & Scott Streets
Telephone 366-7723

Opens October 25
In repertory until
December 11
Evenings 8:30 pm
Saturday Matinees 2 pm
Tickets $5.50-$1.50

by Bertolt Brecht
English version
by Charles Laughton

"One of Brecht's Finest
Masterpieces...
The Epic of a Man who
Shook the Stars"

Design: Gottschalk + Ash Ltd

⑨ Design Canada

XIV Triennale
di Milano

XIV Triennale,
Milan

XIVe Triennale
de Milan

XIV. Mailänder
Triennale

15 maggio al 14 luglio,1968 May 15 to July 14,1968 15 mai au 14 juillet 1968 15.Mai bis 14.Juli 1968

Rolf Harder, Design Collaborative

Produced by the Department of
Industry, Trade and Commerce, Ottawa,
and the National Design Council

Publié par le ministère de l'Industrie
et du Commerce, Ottawa, et le Conseil national
de l'esthétique industrielle

Design Canada

Management of Design
The new better business philosophy

La gestion du design
La nouvelle philosophie des affaires

Canada   **Ernst Roch**   1977   Traveling exhibition of the work
of the two designers
23½" × 33"

Exhibition
of Graphic Design by
Rolf Harder and Ernst Roch
Design Collaborative

Art Gallery of York University
in collaboration with the
Goethe-Institut Toronto
9 February to 28 February 1979

Exposition
de design graphique de
Rolf Harder et Ernst Roch
Design Collaborative

Art Gallery of York University
en collaboration avec le
Goethe-Institut Toronto
9 février au 28 février 1979

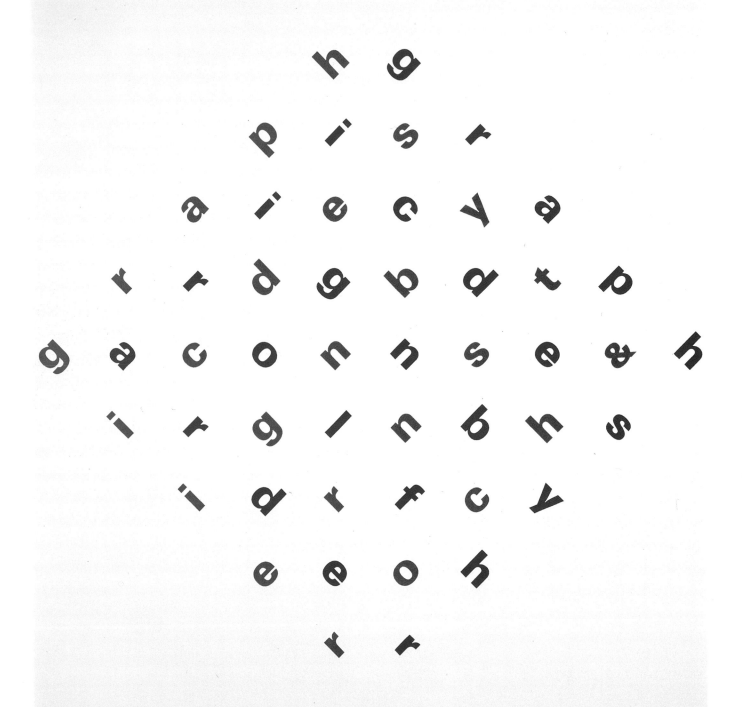

Exhibition
of Graphic Design by
Rolf Harder and Ernst Roch
Design Collaborative

Art Gallery of York University
in collaboration with the
Goethe-Institut Toronto
9 February to 28 February 1979

Exposition
de design graphique de
Rolf Harder et Ernst Roch
Design Collaborative

Art Gallery of York University
en collaboration avec le
Goethe-Institut Toronto
9 février au 28 février 1979

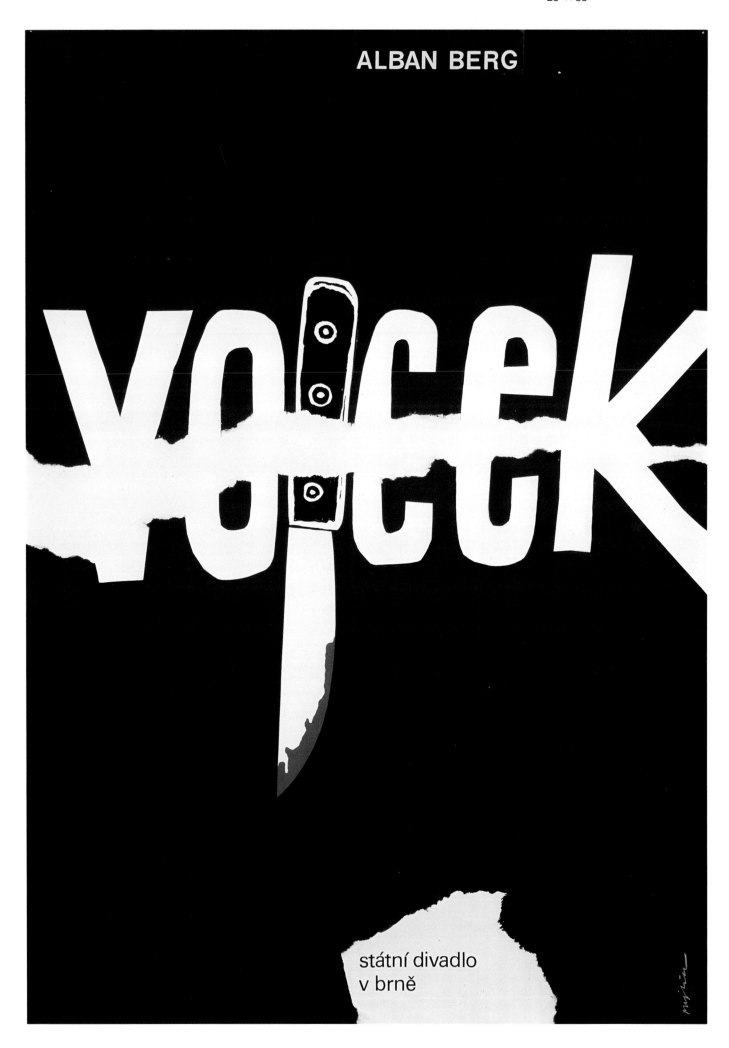

Galéria hlavného mesta SSR Bratislavy Kultúrne leto '81

ZÁHRADNÁ
KERAMIKA
3 / 81
Letná čitáreň
Červený
rak

GMB

Mestská jún
knižnica –august
v Bratislave 1981

IMRICH
VANEK

design © Rostoka NVB 140/81

MUSEUM OF MODERN ART NEW YORK : ILLUMS BOLIGHUS KØBENHAVN

MAINOSGRAAFIKOT RY 25 VUOTTA KÄYTTÖGRAFIIKKAA
NÄYTTELY FINLANDIA–TALOSSA 2–7.11.1978
LAHDEN TAIDEMUSEOSSA 26.10.–19.11.1978

Martti A Mykkänen/Paino Amer-Yhtymä Oy Kiviranta 1978

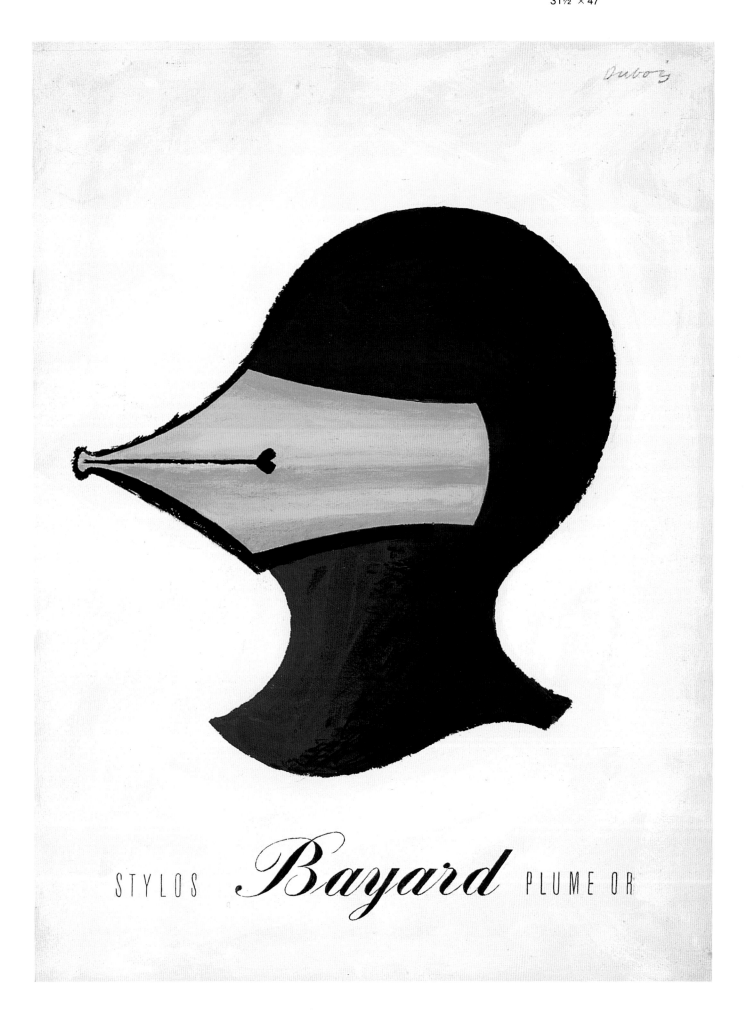

ADMINISTRATION DES MONNAIES & MÉDAILLES

OUVERTURE
AU 1er JUILLET 1985
DE LA NOUVELLE
GALERIE DE VENTE
2 RUE GUÉNÉGAUD
PARIS 75006

MONNAIE DE PARIS

11 QUAI DE CONTI, PARIS 6e

musée : ouverture du lundi au samedi inclus de 11 h à 17 h (sauf jours fériés)

visite guidée des ateliers : lundi et mercredi entre 14 h 15 et 15 h (sauf jours fériés) suspendues du 1er juillet au 15 septembre

galerie de vente : ouverture du lundi au vendredi de 9 h à 17 h 45 (sauf jours fériés), le samedi de 9 h à 11 h 45

France   **Jean Widmer**   1980   City of Kiel
International sailing competition
16" × 33"

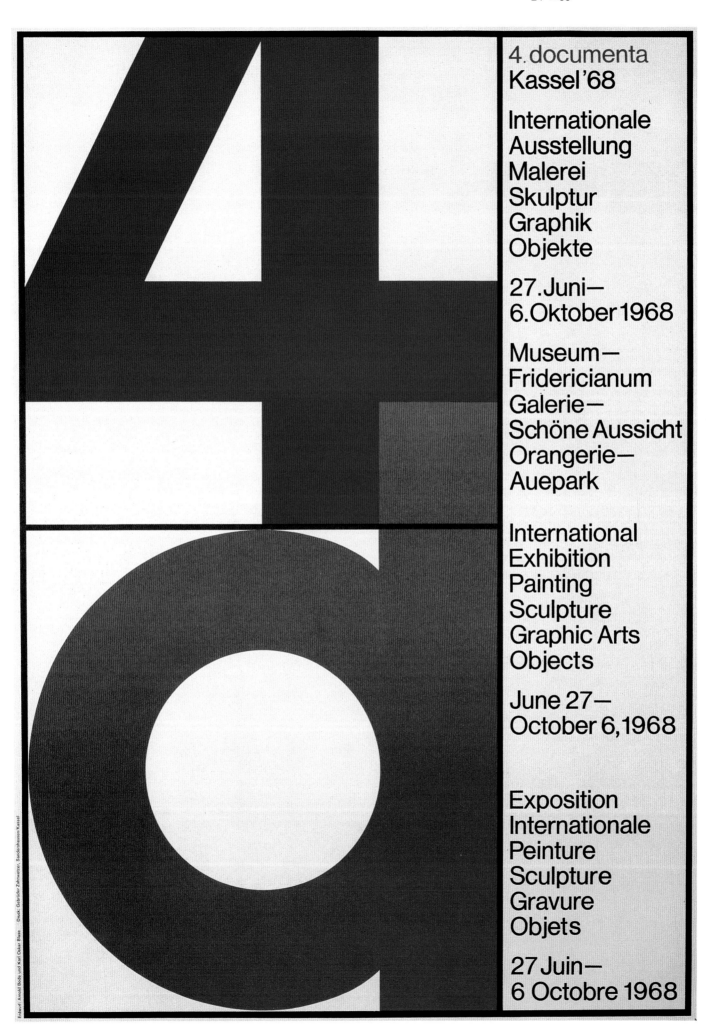

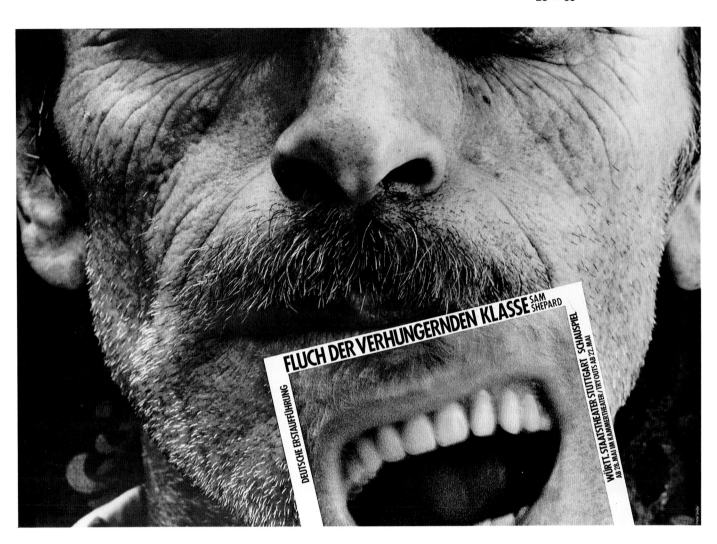

Volkskunst
aus
Mazedonien

**Forum
für
Kulturaustausch**

**Ausstellung
vom 29. September
bis   29. Oktober
Di–Fr 11.00–19.00
Sa/So 11.00–17.00
Mo geschlossen
Eintritt frei**

**Institut
für
Auslandsbeziehungen**

**Stuttgart
Charlottenplatz 17
(Planieseite)**

Volkskunst
Mazedonien

Design Hans Peter Hoch
Siebdruck Scherer

Internationales
Design
Zentrum
Berlin e.V.

Design im Dialog

Design ist Kommunikation
Kommunikation ist Teilhaben.

Mehr Kommunikation und
mehr Teilhaben
verbessern die Voraussetzungen
des guten Design.

Design im Dialog weiterentwickeln:
Design als Mittel
zur Gestaltung einer auf
den Menschen bezogenen Umwelt.

IDZ

Partner und Initiator
dieses Dialogs sein,
ist die zentrale Aufgabe
des IDZ.

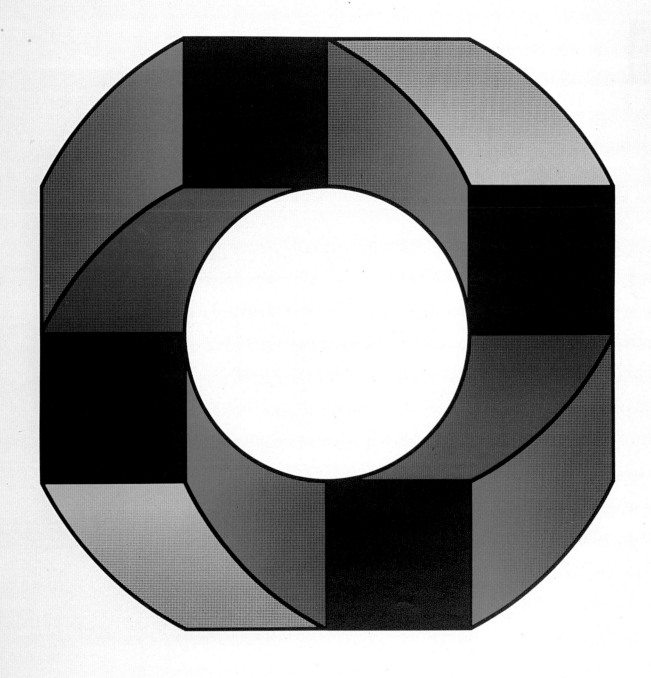

H W Kapitzki IVKD b-1-co siebdruck

West Germany   **Isolde Monson-Baumgart**   1978   Film
"A trip to Vienna"
23" × 33"

West Germany   **Rolf Müller**   1972   City of Kiel
International sailing competition
33" × 46½"

Kreissparkasse
Esslingen–Nürtingen
1984 – zehn Jahre

Visual Design

Bruno K Wiese

One-man exhibition in Kiel
23" × 33"

SMALL PAINTINGS & DRAWINGS

Letchworth Museum and Art Gallery

15 July - 5 August, Mondays - Thursdays 10.00 - 17.30, Fridays Saturdays 10.00 - 18.00

An Arts Council Exhibition. Admission free. Closed Sundays

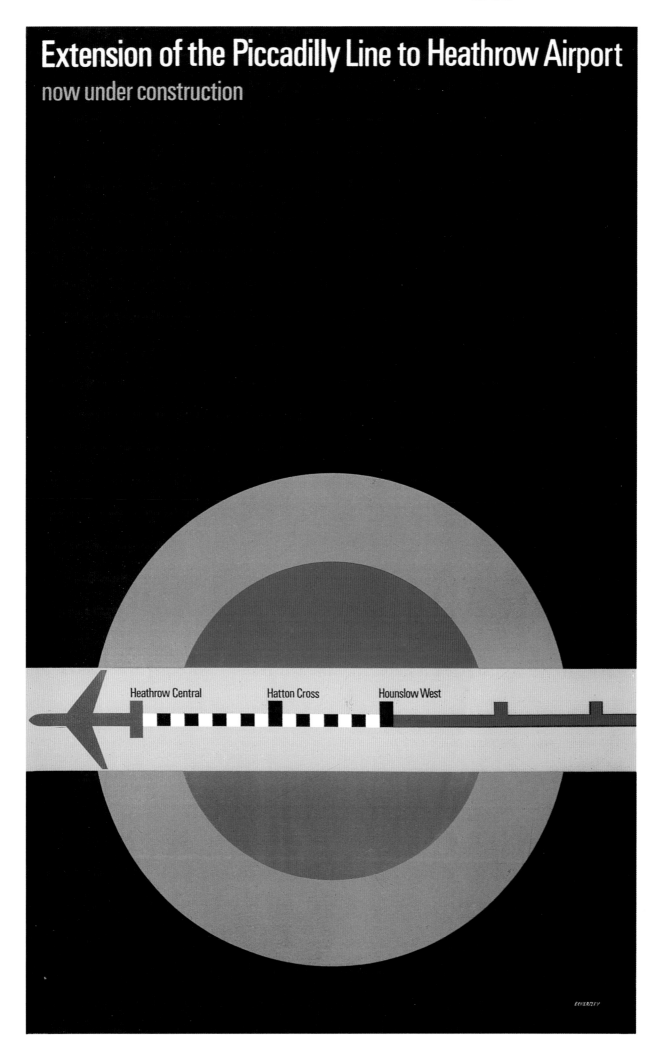

Great Britain   **Alan Fletcher**   1982   Designers Saturday in London
Sponsored by furniture
manufacturers
23'' × 33''

Great Britain   **John Gorham**   1983   Torquay Tourist Board
To promote tourism to the
English Riviera
20" × 30"

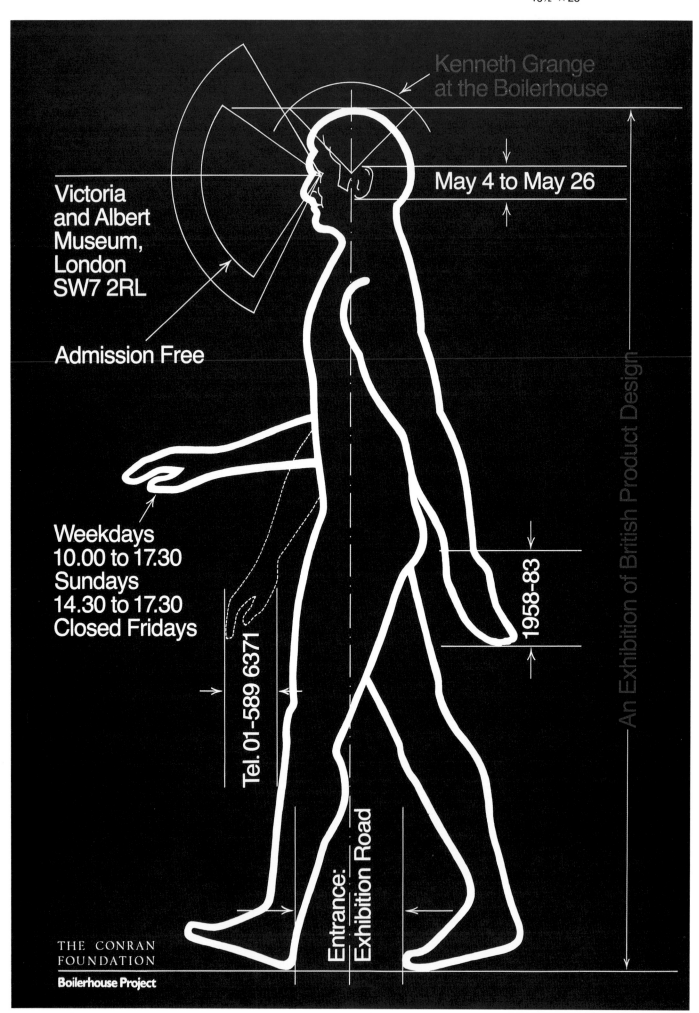

FOUR LECTURES IN JUNE
BY NEIL LEVINE

MONDAY 2ND 7.00PM : BACKGROUND TO WRIGHT'S ACTIVITIES
TUESDAY 3RD 7.00PM : THE ICONOGRAPHY OF HOLLYHOCK HOUSE AND CALIFORNIA
WEDNESDAY 4TH 7.00PM : FALLING WATER AND DIAGONAL PLANNING IN THE 20'S AND 30'S
THURSDAY 5TH NOON : FROM TALIESIN WEST TO THE GUGGENHEIM MUSEUM, THE SPIRAL OF TIME
THE LECTURE HALL, THE ARCHITECTURAL ASSOCIATION 34-36 BEDFORD SQUARE LONDON WC1 TEL 636 0974

Un Nouveau Service Couleur
Pour la réalisation de toutes vos maquettes finalisées en une ou plusieurs
couleurs, conditionnements, étiquettes, PLV, textes, logos...

Mode d'emploi
Commencez par regarder intensément le carré noir supérieur
pendant 30 secondes, puis faites descendre votre regard sur le carré noir inférieur,
dans les espaces blancs l'environnant vous devez apercevoir
de légers cercles de couleur, ces couleurs sont les complémentaires de celles
des deux cercles supérieurs.
Cet effet s'explique simplement. En effet, si vous fixez longuement une couleur,
du rouge par exemple, vos récepteurs oculaires rouges
s'y adaptent, et donc, par réflexion sur un fond blanc on aperçoit ensuite du vert.
Inversement, si vous utilisez un fond noir, l'effet de rouge persiste.

4 rue de Jarente 75004 Paris Tél. 887.53.04

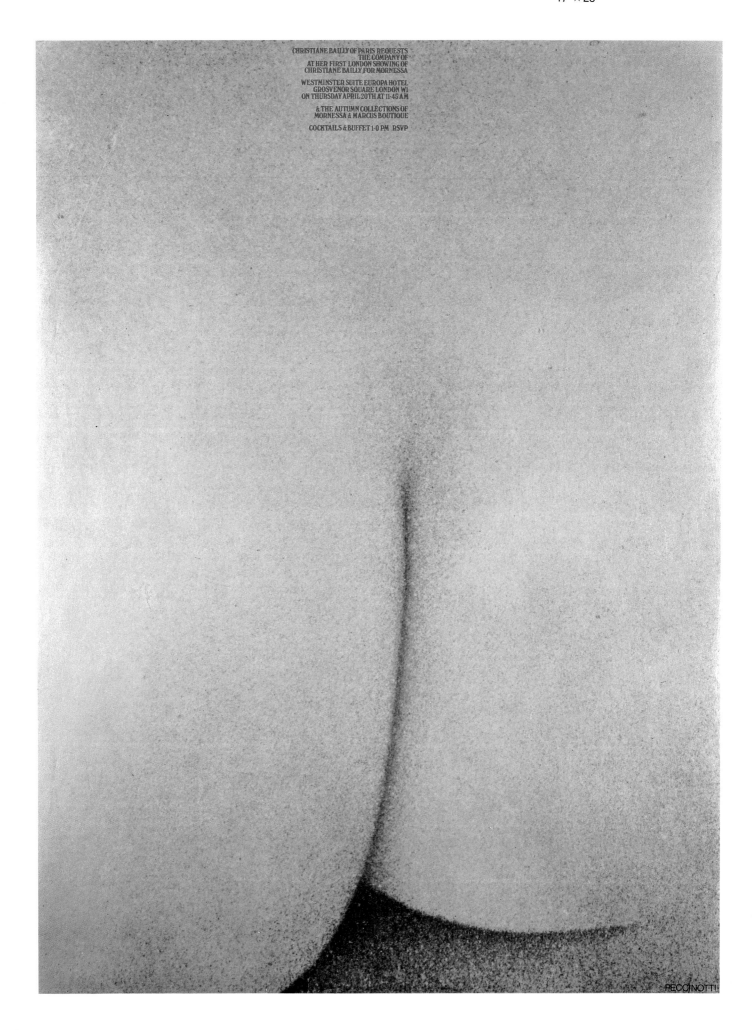

CHRISTIANE BAILLY OF PARIS REQUESTS
THE COMPANY OF
AT HER FIRST LONDON SHOWING OF
CHRISTIANE BAILLY FOR MORNESSA

WESTMINSTER SUITE EUROPA HOTEL
GROSVENOR SQUARE LONDON W1
ON THURSDAY APRIL 20TH AT 11·45 AM

& THE AUTUMN COLLECTIONS OF
MORNESSA & MARCUS BOUTIQUE

COCKTAILS & BUFFET 1·0 PM RSVP

PECCINOTTI

Imperial War Museum
Lambeth Road
London SE1

a new permanent exhibition
on the development of modern warfare
1775-1980

Monday to Saturday 10-5.50
Sunday 2-5.50
Admission free

Underground:
Lambeth North or Elephant & Castle

Designed by Herbert Spencer   Printed by Gavin Martin Ltd

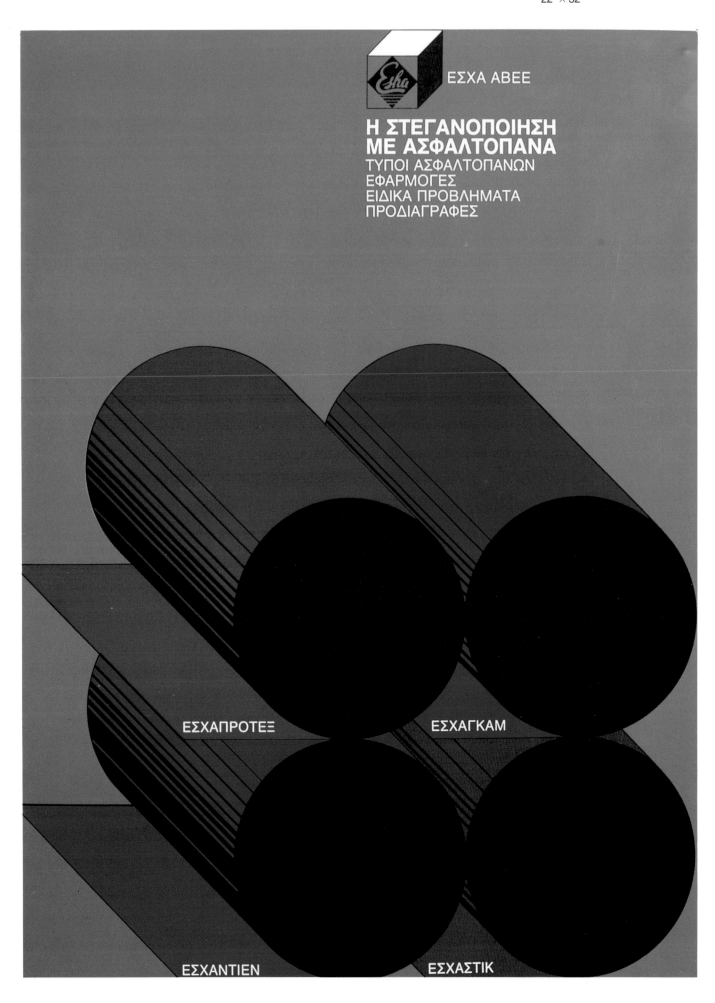

PoppyDay

殘廢軍人籌款

DAN REISINGER
רמזי אובקט אחזים מאוחדים ב.ע.מ

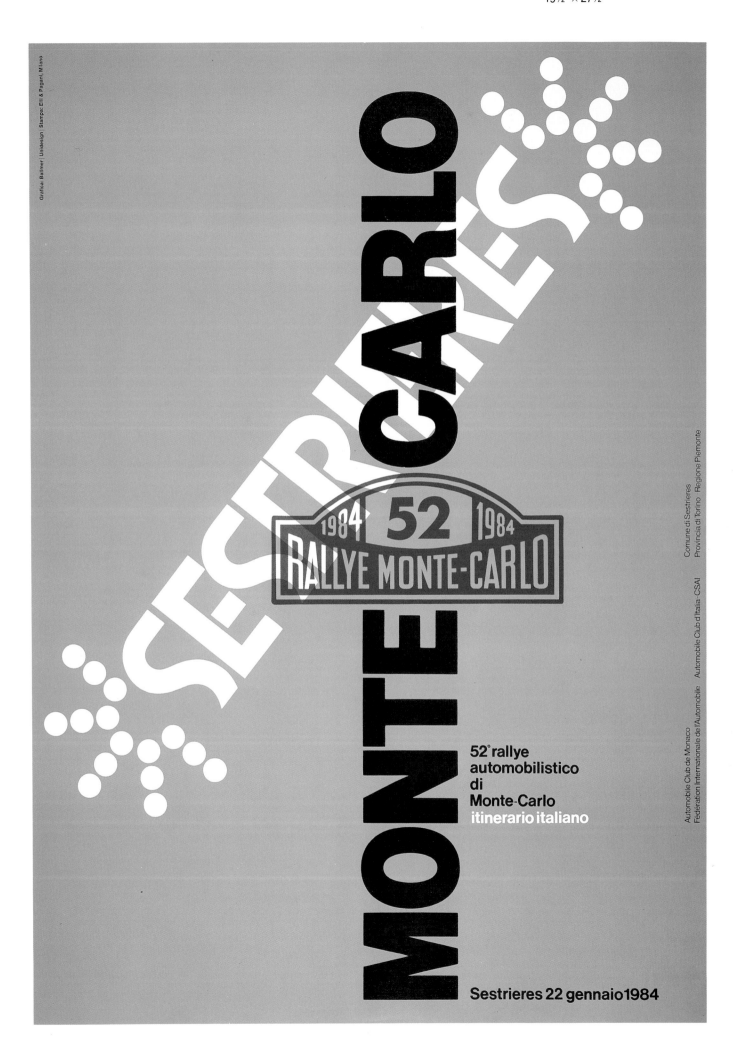

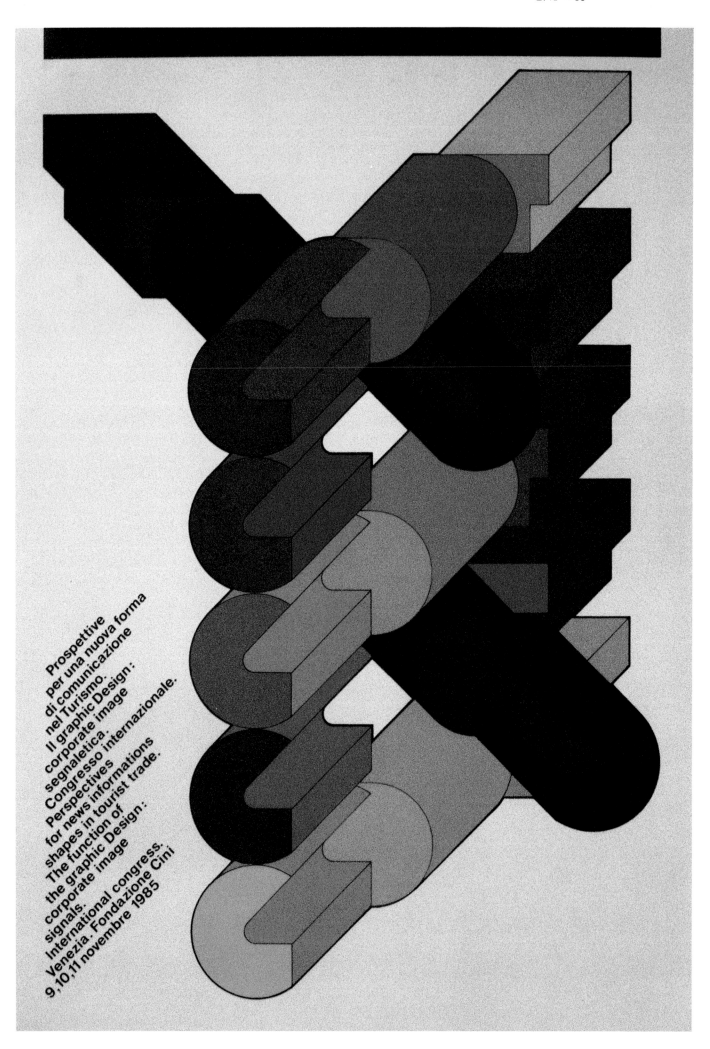

Prospettive
per una nuova forma
di comunicazione
nel Turismo.
Il graphic Design:
corporate image
segnaletica.
Congresso internazionale.
Perspectives
for news informations
shapes in tourist trade.
The function of
the graphic Design:
corporate image
signals.
International congress.
Venezia. Fondazione Cini
9,10,11 novembre 1985

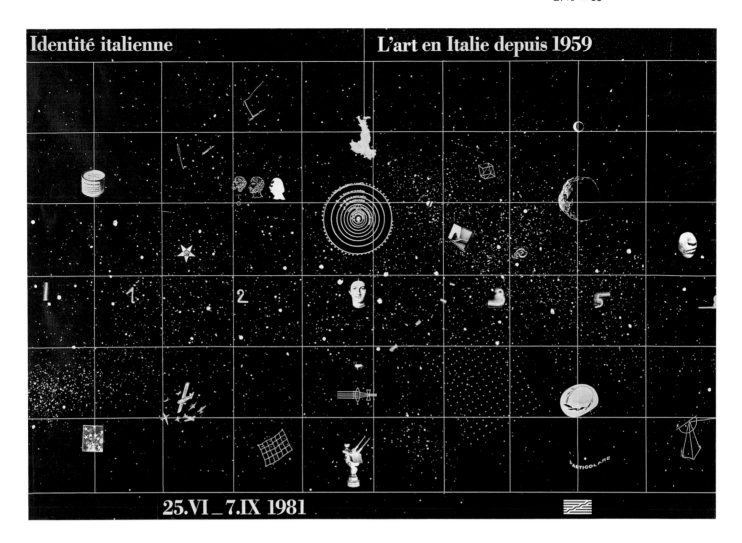

SERIE SEGNO/PAROLA - COMUNICAZIONE TRA SILVIO COPPOLA E LUIGI VERONELLI SU: IN OGNI BICCHIERE DI VINO UN'IMMAGINE DI GIOVANE DONNA - ART DIRECTOR SILVIO COPPOLA - EDITORI PAOLO BELLASICH E ROBERTO BOSSI - MILANO

Italy

Franco Grignani

1983

Exhibition
"Visual Design 1933–1983"
Milan
16½" × 23½"

0
1
L'immagine raggiunge la sua dinamica
L'esperimento è il risultato di un conflitto fra forze esterne ed interne, fra forze dinamiche e forze di riferimento. / franco.grignani
2
3
4
5
6
7
8
9
10
unità per mezzo di vari livelli di integrazione: tensione, ritmo, armonia matematica.

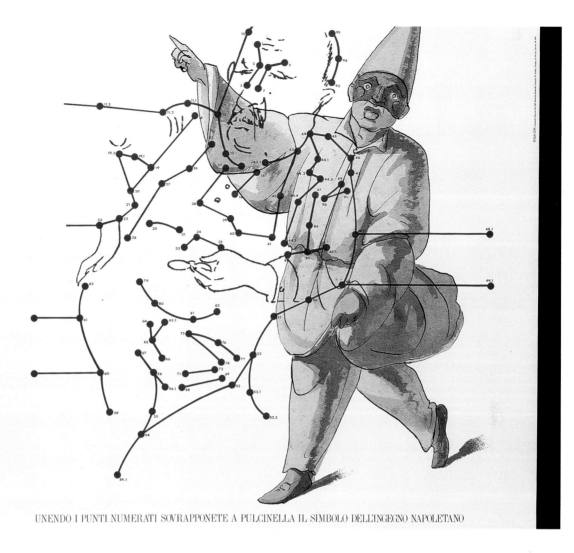

Manifesto commissionato
dalla Fondazione Napoli '39
come contributo per una
nuova immagine culturale
della città

UNENDO I PUNTI NUMERATI SOVRAPPONETE A PULCINELLA IL SIMBOLO DELL'INGEGNO NAPOLETANO

Italy   **Bob Noorda**   1978   50th anniversary of *Domus* magazine
                                                                      10,000 architects, designers,
                                                                      artists and authors are listed
                                                                      17" × 24"

domus
50 anni
di architettura,
design, arte

50 years
of architecture,
design, art

50 ans
d'architecture,
design, art

Roberto Sambonet   da   Piero della Francesca

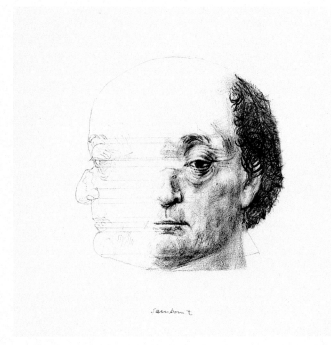

Roberto Sambonet   da   Piero della Francesca

per BRERA

Exhibition
100 designers
The Triennale Milan
27½" × 39"

mostra ufficiale del congresso
ICSID 1983
Triennale di Milano
"dal cucchiaio alla città
nell'itinerario
di 100 designers"
Milano, 23 ottobre 1983
ADI Assarredo Comune di Milano
in collaborazione con
Philip Morris
Abet Laminati Centro Ricerche
Acerbis/Stoppino
Alchimia
Emilio Ambasz
Antonia Astori
Antonio Barrese
Carlo Bartoli
BBPR
Mario Bellini
Beppe Benenti
Cini Boeri
Rodolfo Bonetto
Guy Bonsiepe
Andrea Branzi
Bruce Burdick
Anna Castelli Ferrieri
Clino Castelli
Achille Castiglioni
Centrokappa
Centro Ricerche Pininfarina
Centro Progetti Technico
Citterio A./Nava P.
Silvio Coppola
Angelo Cortesi
Da Centro per il disegno Ambientale
Riccardo Dalisi
Paolo Deganello
Design Group
D'Urbino Lomazzi De Pas
Ulrich Franzen
Gianfranco Frattini
Anna Maria Fundaró
Giorgetto Giugiaro
Gramigna Mazza
Michael Graves
Makio Hasuike
Hans Hollein
Isao Hosoe
ISIA Firenze
ISIA Roma
Arata Isozaki
Douglas Kelley
Hans Von Klier
Shiro Kuramata
Gerd Lange
Ugo La Pietra
L/O Design Lucci & Orlandini
Sasa Machtig
Vico Magistretti
Angelo Mangiarotti
Enzo Mari
Alessandro Mendini
Richard Meyer
Mid Design
Pierluigi Molinari
Massimo Morozzi
Giulia Moselli
Bruno Munari
Paola Navone
George Nelson
Neumeister Design
Antti Nurmesniemi
Open Ark
David Palterer
Pentagram Design
Gaetano Pesce
Renzo Piano
Giancarlo Piretti
Paolo Piva
Charles Pollock
Paolo Portoghesi
Franco Raggi
Aldo Rossi
David Rowland
Claudio Salocchi
Roberto Sambonet
Denys Santachiara
Richard Sapper
Tobia Scarpa
Fratelli Shakespear
Sottsass Associati
Giotto Stoppino
Pierluigi Spadolini
Nanni Strada
Studio Albini-Helg-Piva
Studio Nizzoli
Superstudio
Kazuhide Takahama
Trabucco e Vecchi
Oscar Tusquets
Unimark International
Aldo Van Den Nieuvelaar
Andries Van Onck
Carla Venosta
Robert Venturi
Massimo Vignelli
Nanda Vigo
Daniel Weil
Yrjo Wiherheimo
Marco Zanuso
design
Heinz Waibl
sponsor del manifesto
Nava Milano spa

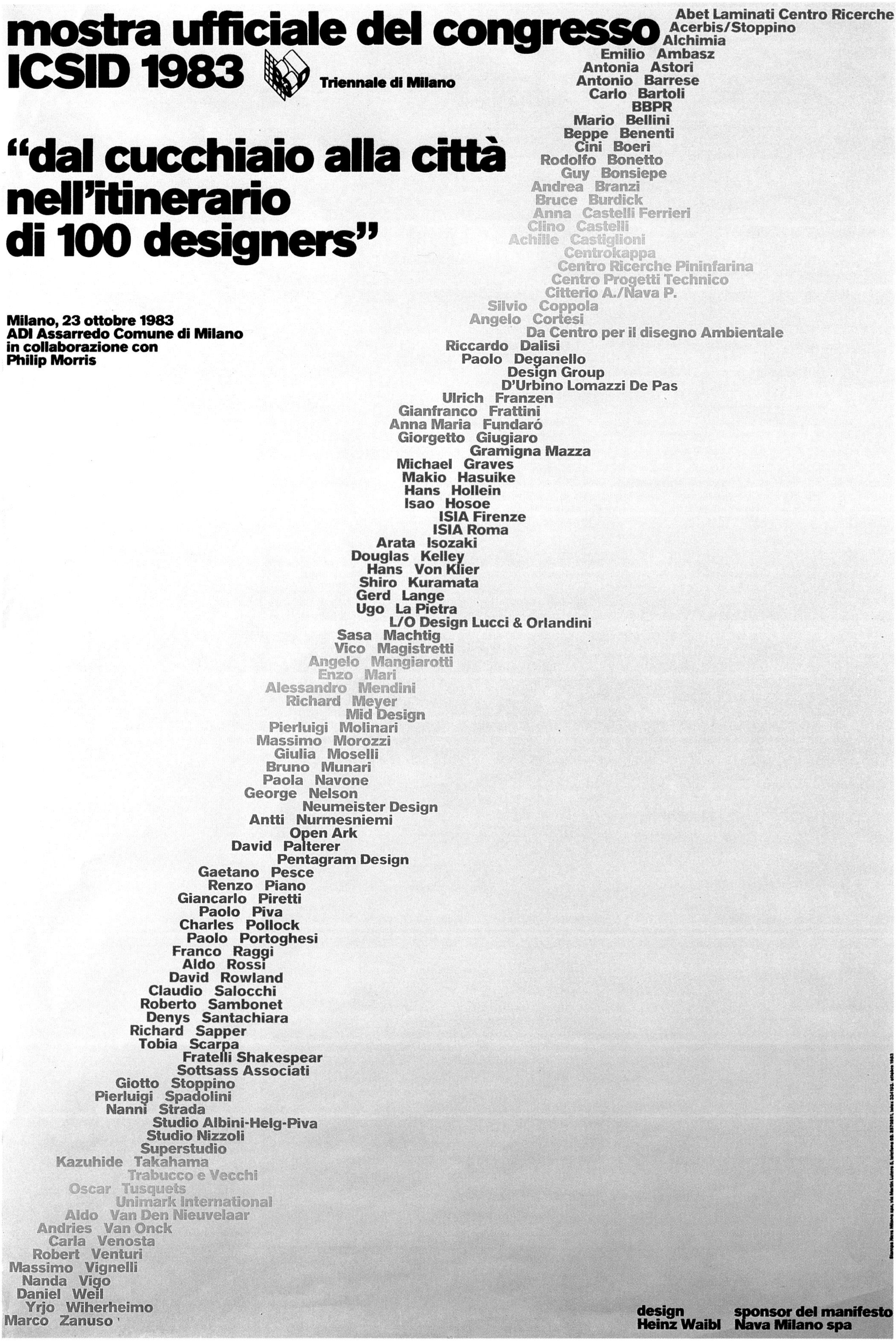

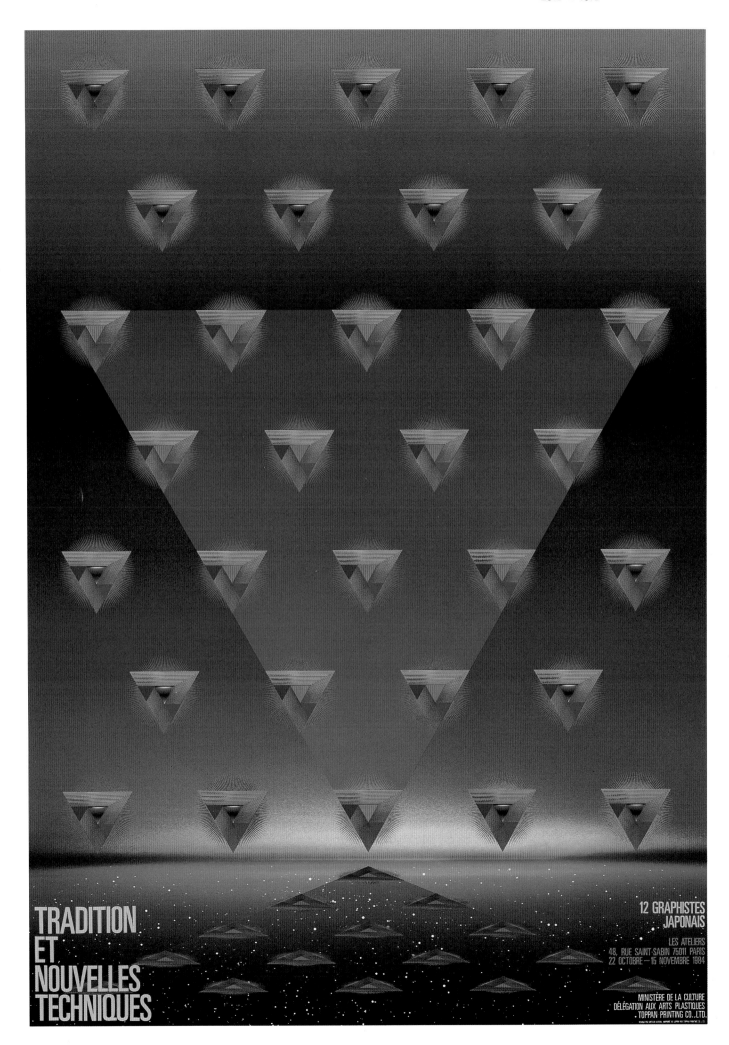

永井一正の世界展 8月1日金 — 11月30日日 池田二十世紀美術館 静岡県伊東市一碧湖畔

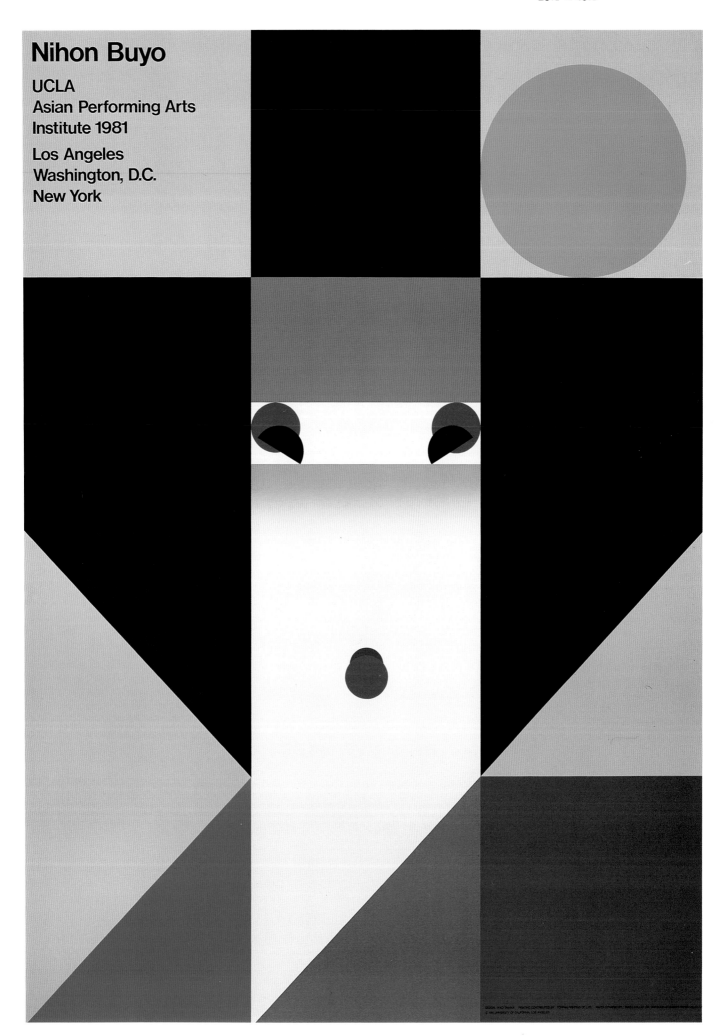

Nihon Buyo

UCLA
Asian Performing Arts
Institute 1981

Los Angeles
Washington, D.C.
New York

Nihon Buyo

UCLA
Asian Performing Arts
Institute 1981

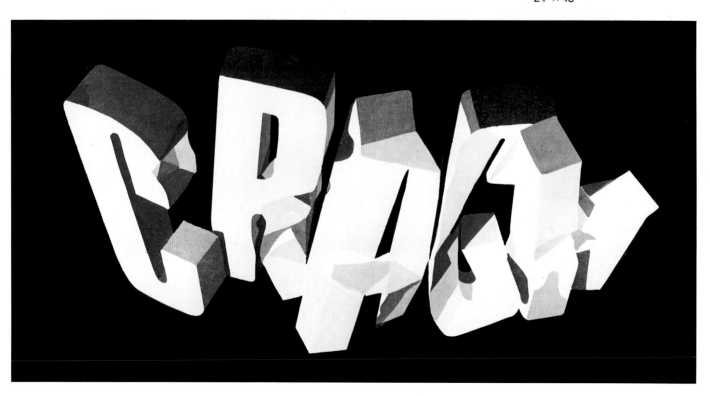

**ook voor
uitzendkrachten**
recht op vakantie
vakantiebijslag
geld voor feestdagen
en voor kort verzuim

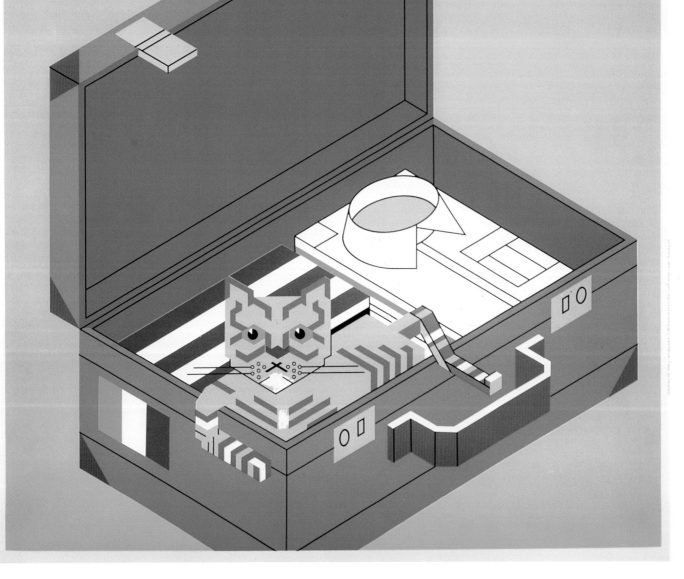

panamarenko

rijksmuseum kröller-müller, otterlo
27 augustus tot 16 oktober 1978

zwarte beertjes

zakboeken

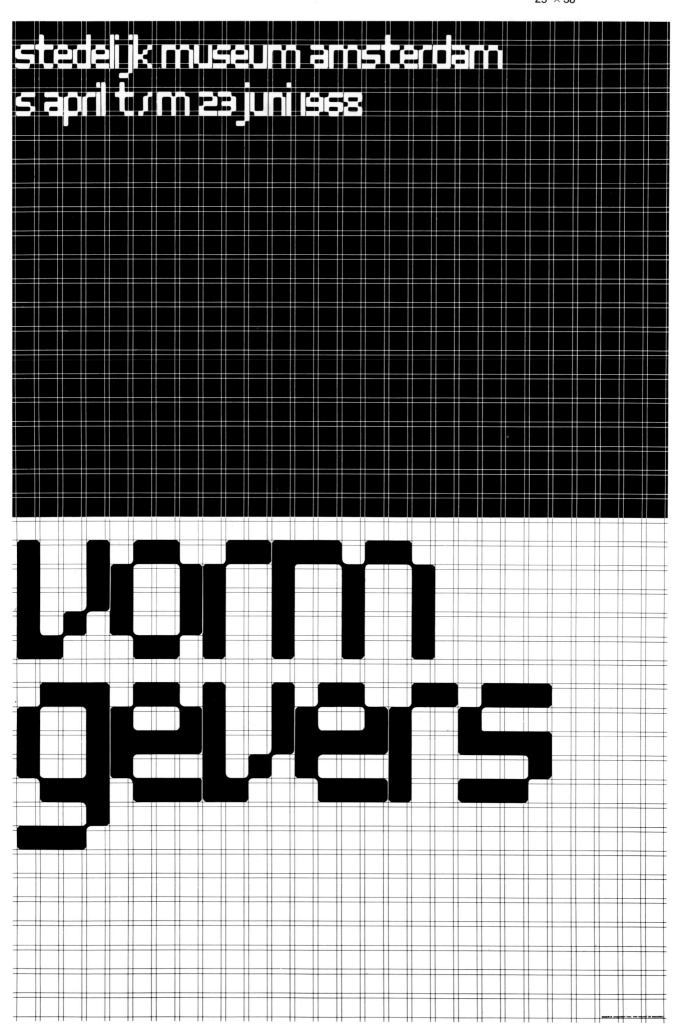

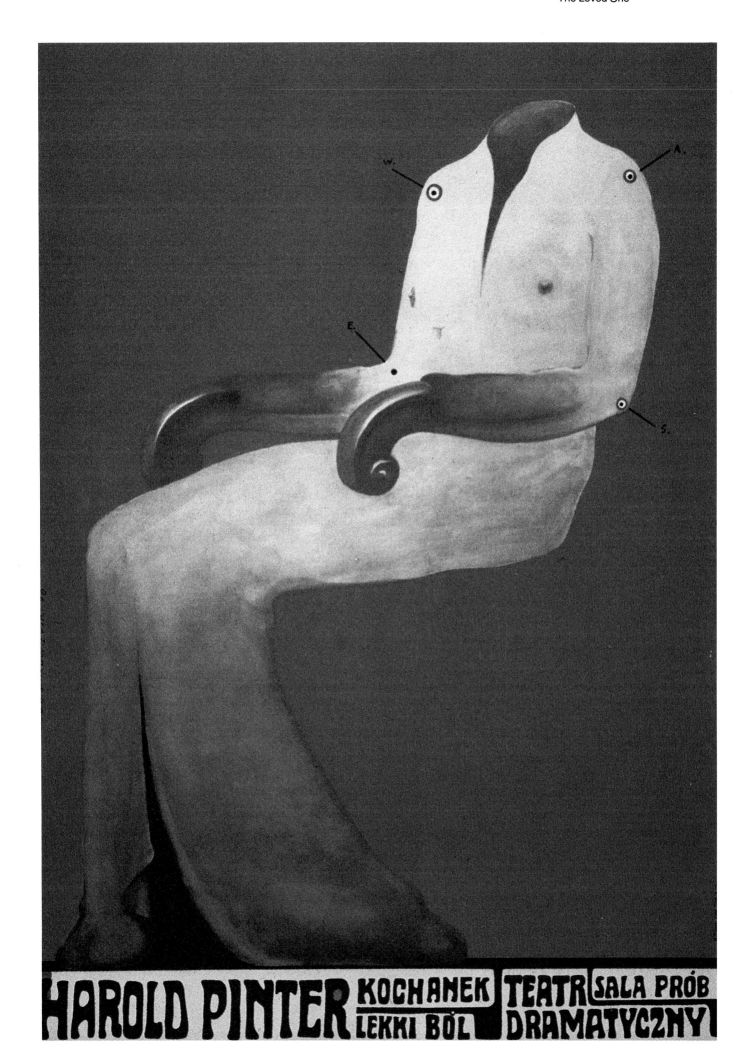

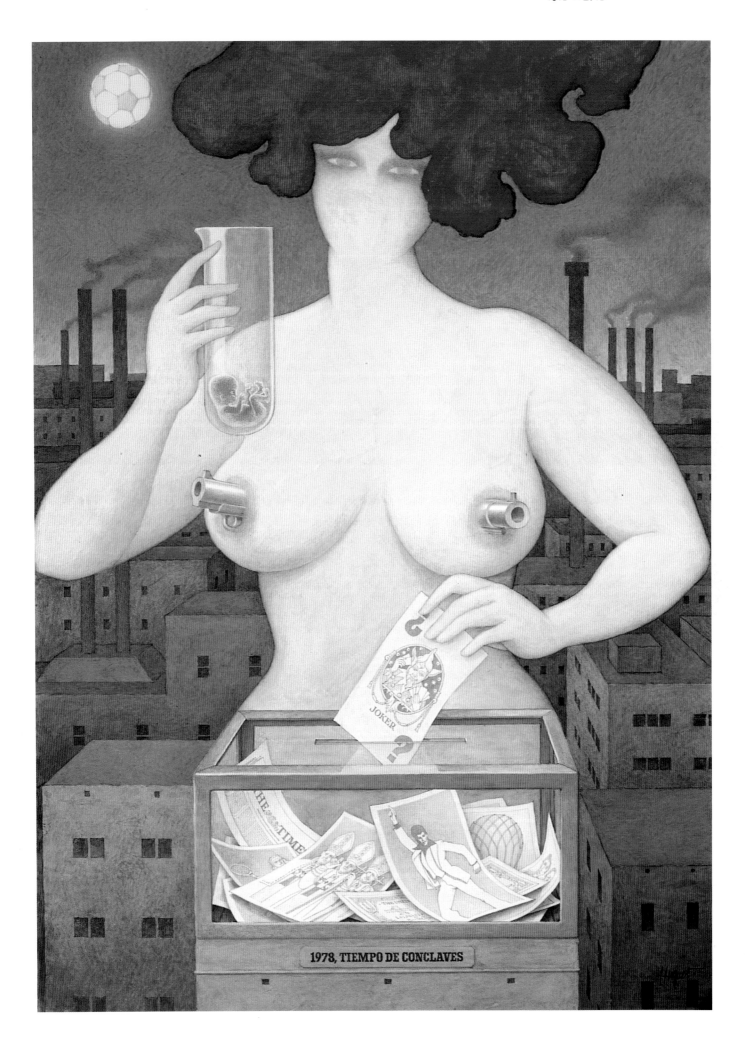

I M A G I N A L A P A Z E N E L M U N D O
I M A G G I N N A L A P A Z
I M A G I N A

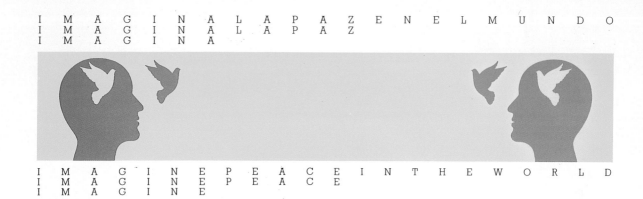

I M A G I N E P E A C E I N T H E W O R L D
I M A G G I N N E E P E A C E E
I M A G I N E E P E A C E

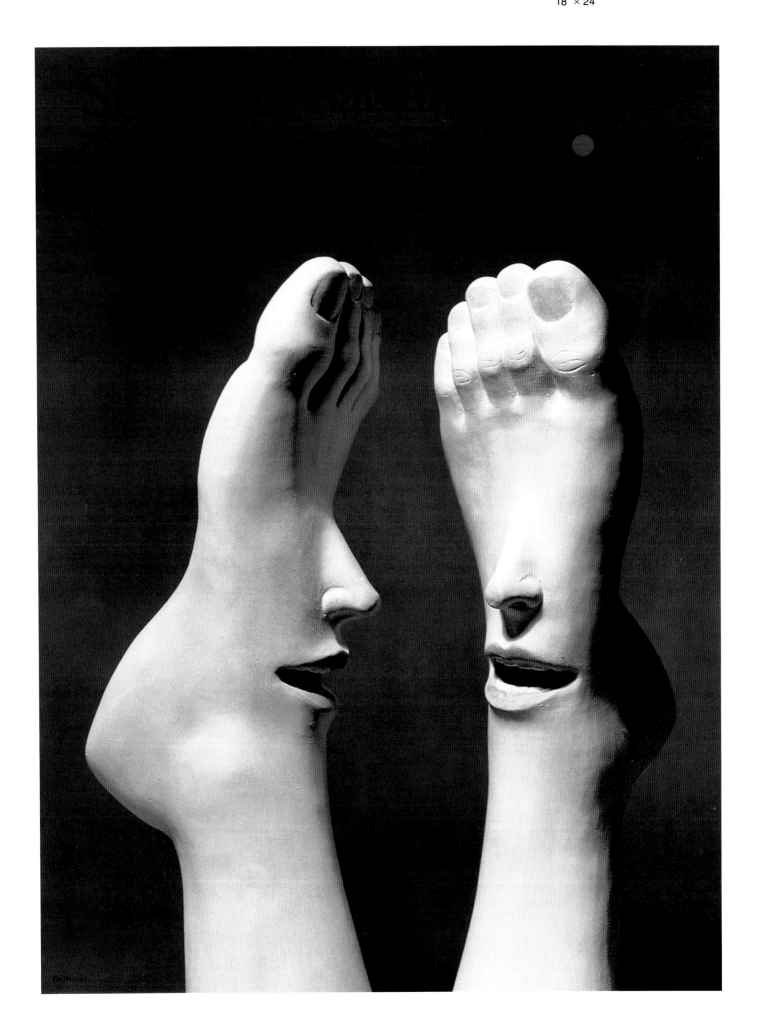

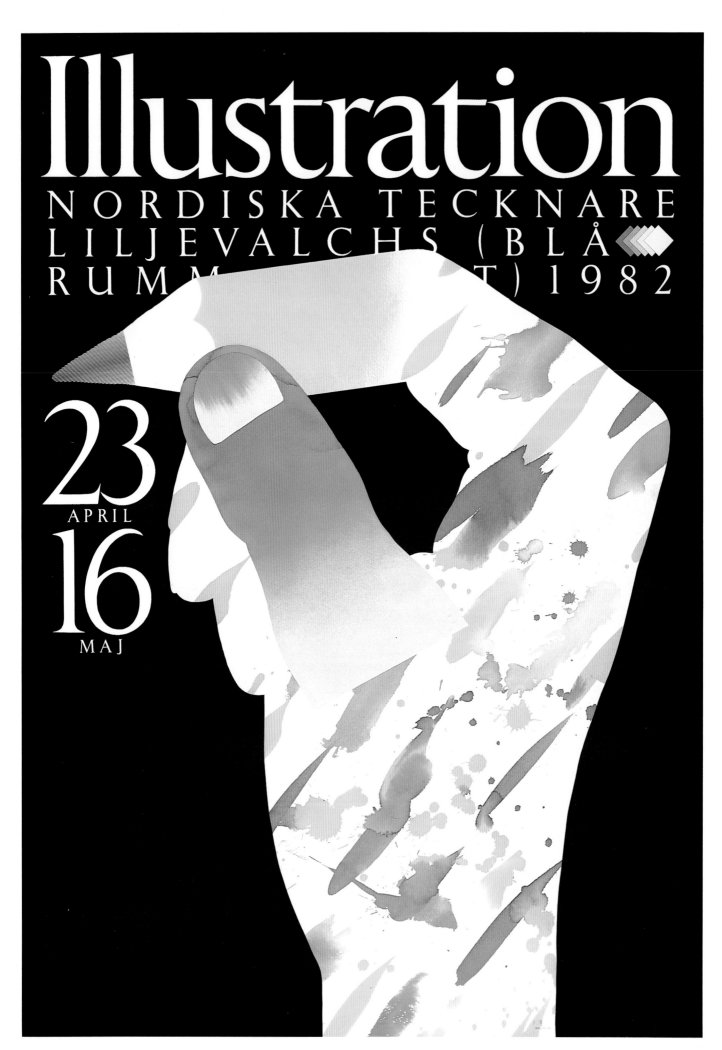

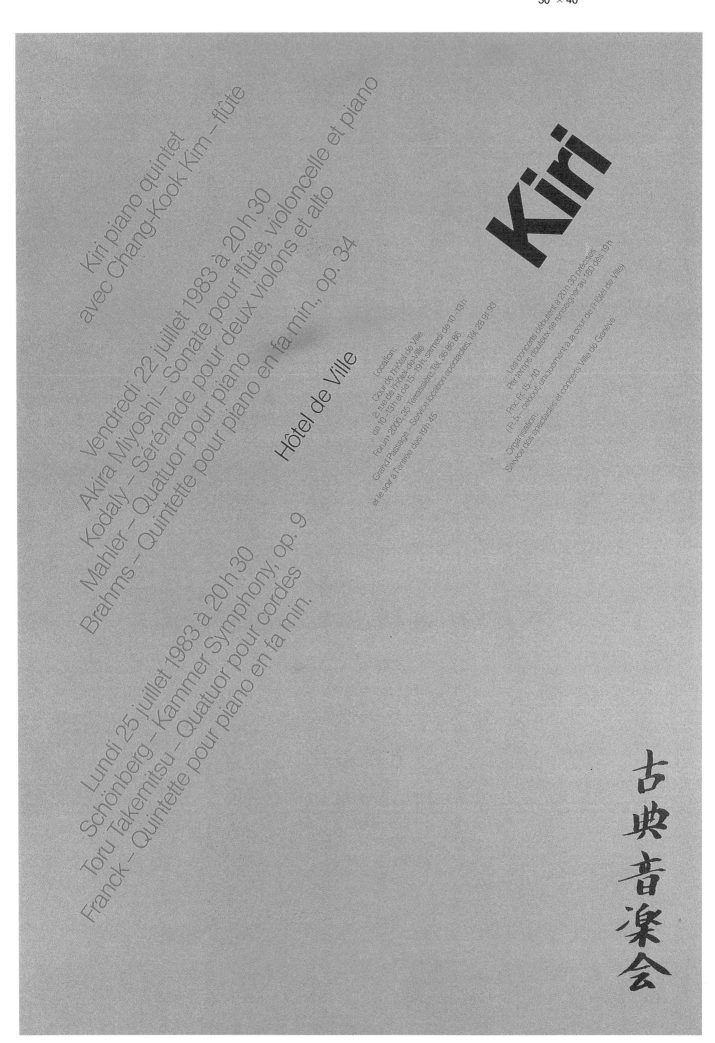

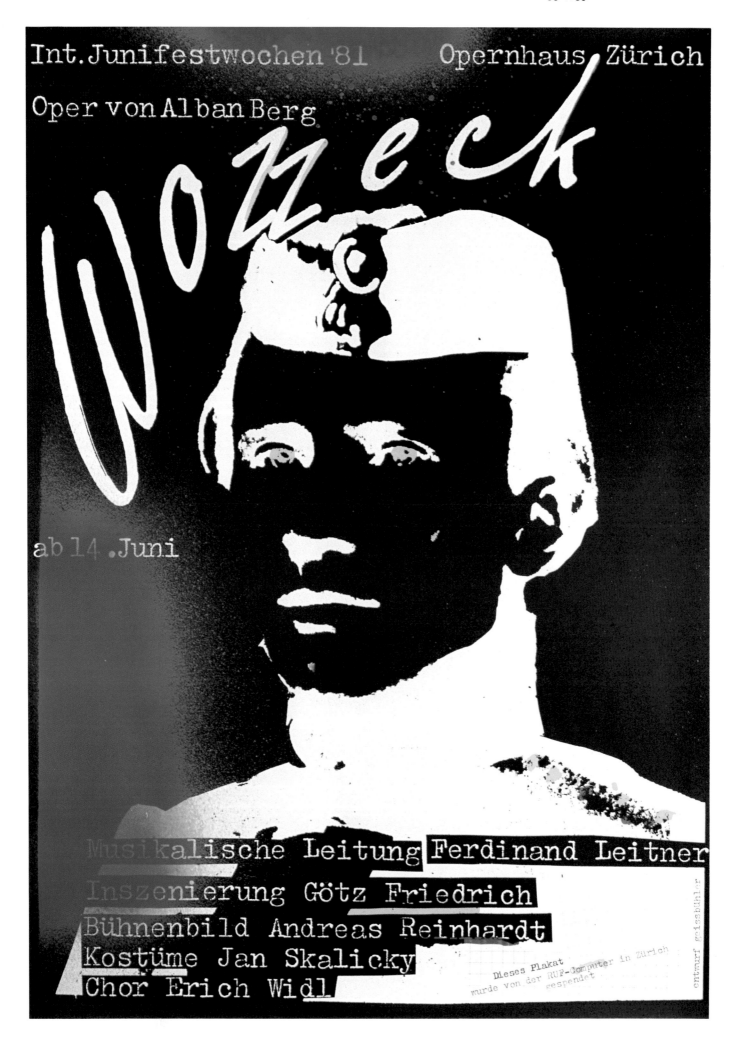

1984

Kieler Woche
16.-24. Juni

galerie aktuell
bern
gerechtigkeitsgasse 23   di bis do bis fr, 16 bis 18.30 uhr
do 20 bis 22 uhr, sa 15 bis 17 uhr
konkrete fotografie   haus teo jakob
4 aspekte

roger humbert
rené mächler
rolf schroeder
j. frédéric schnyder

vom 14. januar bis 15. februar 1967

peter megert mdv / serigraphie albin uldry

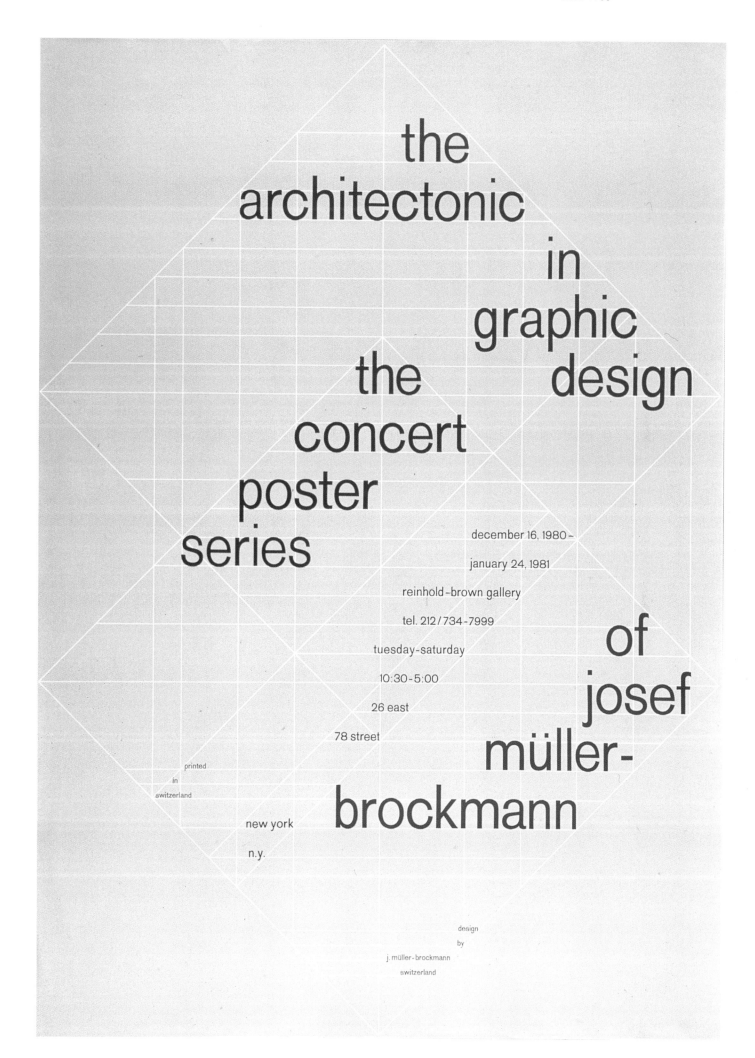

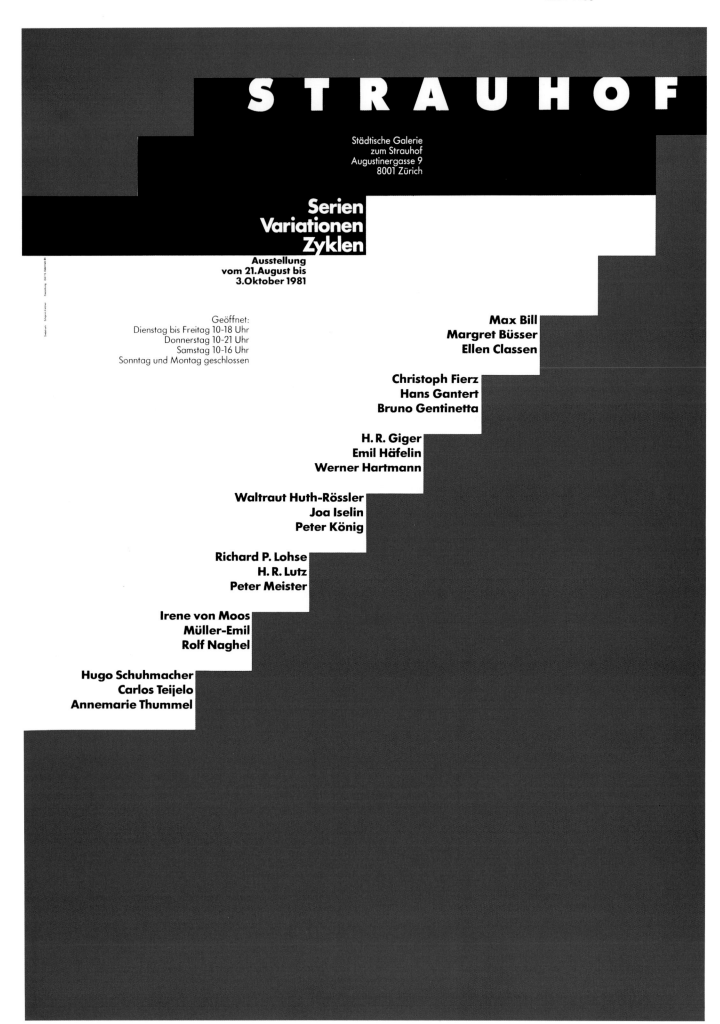

STRAUHOF

Städtische Galerie
zum Strauhof
Augustinergasse 9
8001 Zürich

**Serien
Variationen
Zyklen**

**Ausstellung
vom 21. August bis
3. Oktober 1981**

Geöffnet:
Dienstag bis Freitag 10-18 Uhr
Donnerstag 10-21 Uhr
Samstag 10-16 Uhr
Sonntag und Montag geschlossen

**Max Bill
Margret Büsser
Ellen Classen**

**Christoph Fierz
Hans Gantert
Bruno Gentinetta**

**H. R. Giger
Emil Häfelin
Werner Hartmann**

**Waltraut Huth-Rössler
Joa Iselin
Peter König**

**Richard P. Lohse
H. R. Lutz
Peter Meister**

**Irene von Moos
Müller-Emil
Rolf Naghel**

**Hugo Schuhmacher
Carlos Teijelo
Annemarie Thummel**

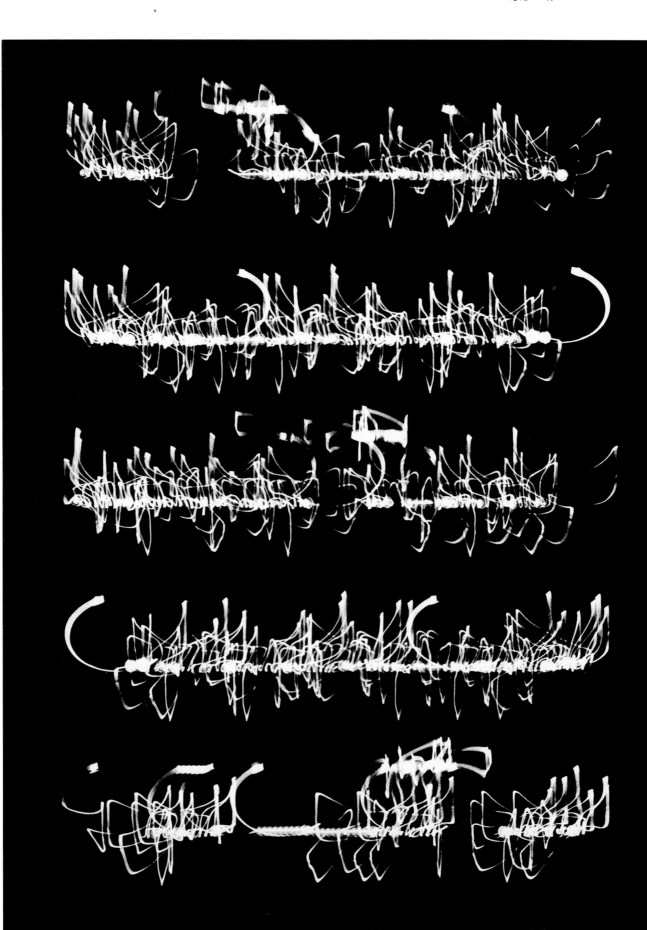

Die Bilder illustrieren die hohe Setzgeschwindigkeit des Composers. Diese hängt davon ab, wie schnell die Schreibkraft maschinenschreiben kann. Der Kugelkopf kann bis zu 14 Anschläge in der Sekunde mithalten. Sekundenschnell geht auch das Auswechseln des Schreibkopfes. Mit einem Handgriff. 53 Schreibelemente aus 5 Schriftfamilien stehen zur Zeit zur Verfügung. Dieser Text wurde auf dem IBM 72 Composer (übrigens von unserer Sekretärin) in der Press Roman, 11 Punkt normal, gesetzt.

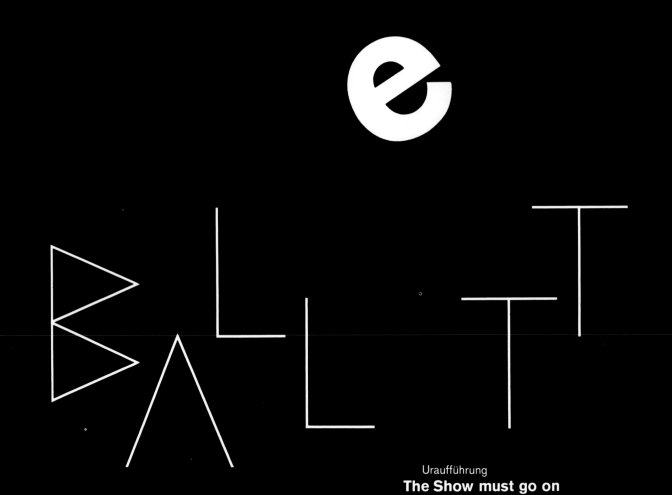

Uraufführung
The Show must go on
Musik von Erwin Nowak und Auszüge aus Werken
von Riccardo Drigo und Ludwig Minkus

Musikalische Leitung: Daniel Lipton
Choreographie: Geoffrey Cauley
Ausstattung: Kaspar Wolfensberger

Premiere
Samstag, 26. April 1975
20 Uhr

Besetzung:
Angelica Bornhausen, Colette Cerf, Gaye Fulton,
Natacha Kelepovska, Susan Kiefer, Helena Villarroya,
Rudolf Budaváry, Ioan Lohan, Joachim Pura,
Marinel Stefanescu, Robert Strajner

Les Biches
Musik von Francis Poulenc

Musikalische Leitung: Daniel Lipton
Choreographie: Bronislava Nijinska
Ausstattung: Marie Laurencin,
bearbeitet von Kaspar Wolfensberger
Einstudierung: Faith Worth
mit Hilfe der Benesh-Dance-Notation

Besetzung:
Colette Cerf, Helena Villarroya
Joachim Pura, Ioan Lohan, Tibor Olah
Simone Fischer, Daniela Fridez
Susanne Bührer, Phillipa Cairne,
Louise Chantelle, Judi Cipriani,
Danielle Dyal, Glynis Gass-Green,
Yvonne Grässle, Sybille Kaess,
Cheryl Mudele, Susan Nye,
Helena Claire Ray, Eve Trachsel

Barbara Bucher, Susanne Bührer,
Phillipa Cairne, Louise Chantelle,
Judi Cipriani, Danielle Dyal,
Simone Fischer, Daniela Fridez,
Glynis Gass-Green, Yvonne Grässle,
Evelyn Harteck, Ruth Harteck,
Sybille Kaess, Beatrix Loehle,
Cheryl Mudele, Susan Nye,   Phillippe Bassat,
Helena Claire Ray, Eve Trachsel   Philipp Beamish,
                                       Pedro De La Cruz,
                                       Stephan Cserhazy,
                                       Tsutomu Iida, Fumio Inagaki,
                                       Yorgos Loukos, Richard Majewski,
                                       Maciej Miedzinski, Mirek Miroslav,
                                       Max Natiez, Tibor Olah,
                                       Jean Francois du Plessis,
Opernhaus Zürich   Dominique de Ribaupierre

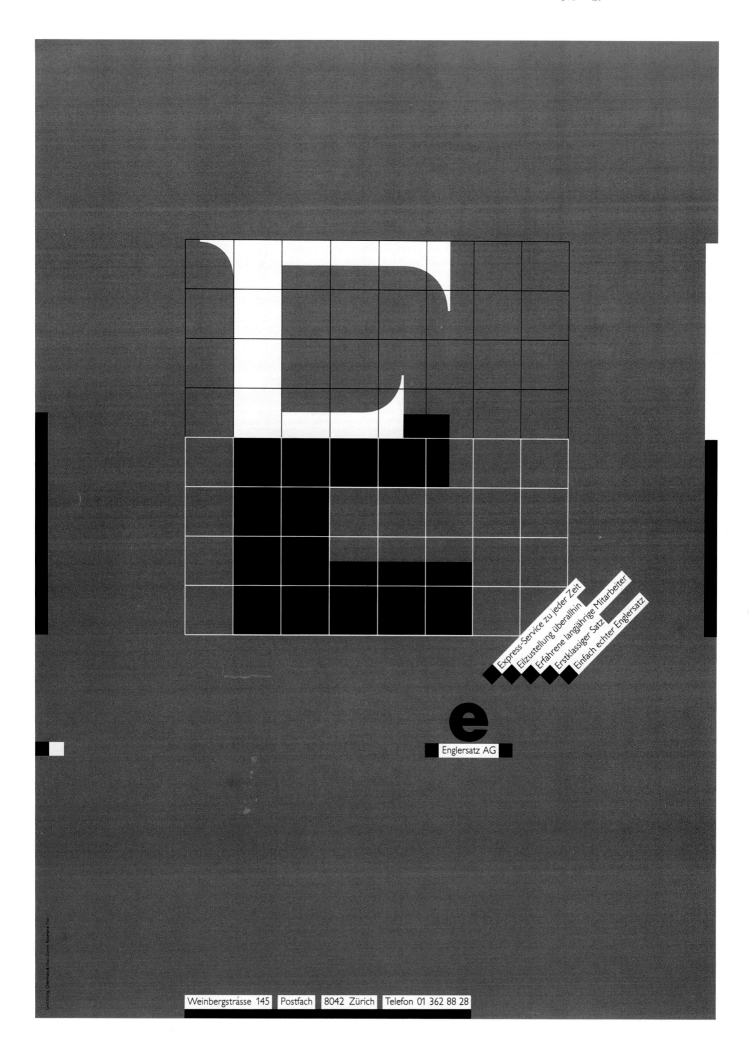

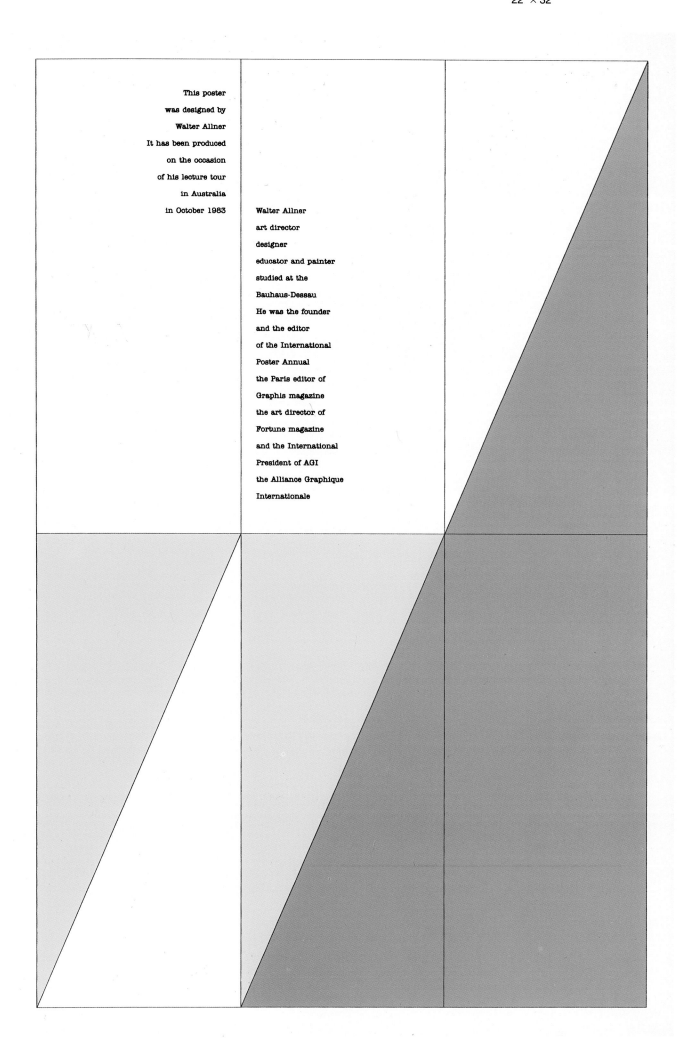

This poster
was designed by
Walter Allner
It has been produced
on the occasion
of his lecture tour
in Australia
in October 1983

Walter Allner
art director
designer
educator and painter
studied at the
Bauhaus-Dessau
He was the founder
and the editor
of the International
Poster Annual
the Paris editor of
Graphis magazine
the art director of
Fortune magazine
and the International
President of AGI
the Alliance Graphique
Internationale

FINE ILLUSTRATED BOOKS IN · THE ARTS · SCIENCES · LITERATURE · ENTERTAINMENT

United States   **Herbert Bayer**   1929   Exhibition of German art
at the Grand Palais Paris
18'' × 24''

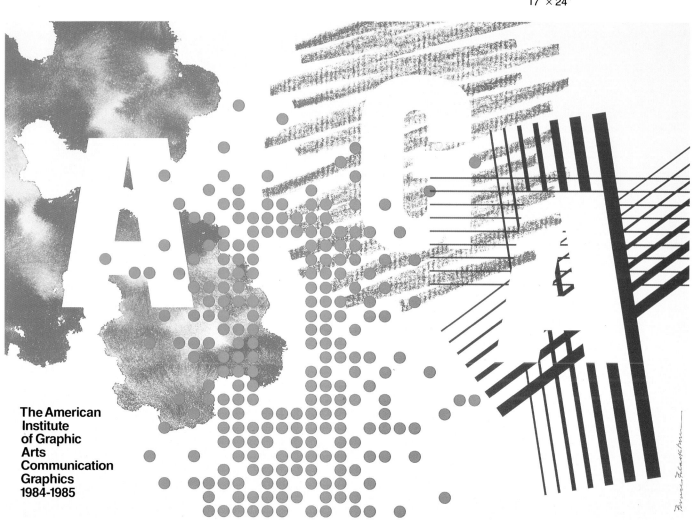

**The American
Institute
of Graphic
Arts
Communication
Graphics
1984-1985**

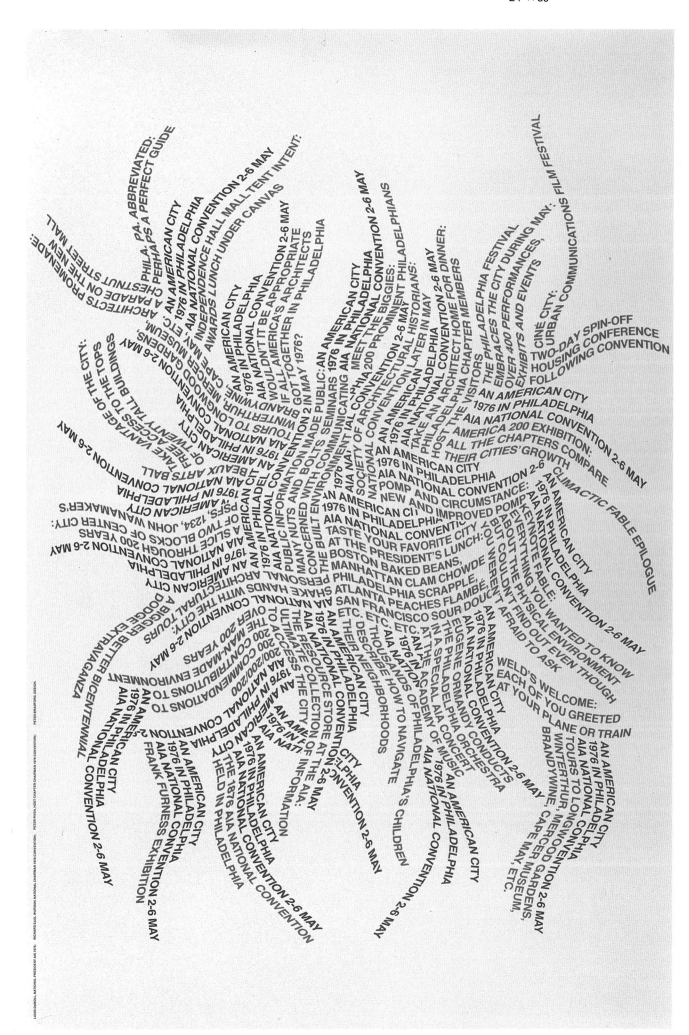

United States **Jacqueline S. Casey** 1967 Exhibition of kinetic sculpture
MIT Committee on the Visual Arts
19½'' × 25½''

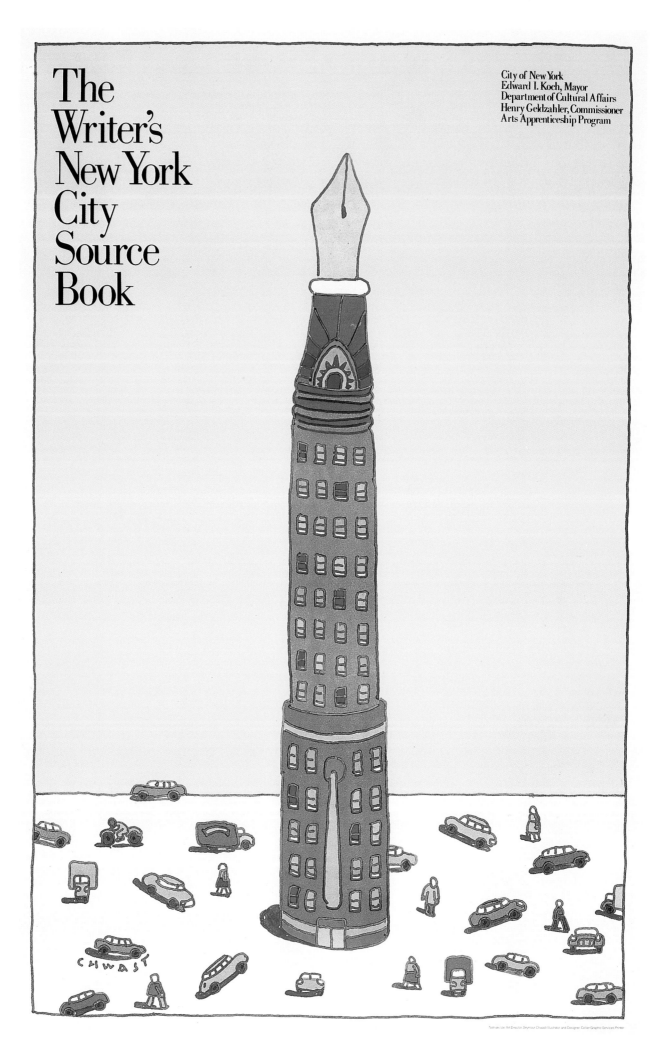

United States	**James Cross**	1985	40th anniversary of
the bombing of Hiroshima
Shoshin Society
24" × 35"

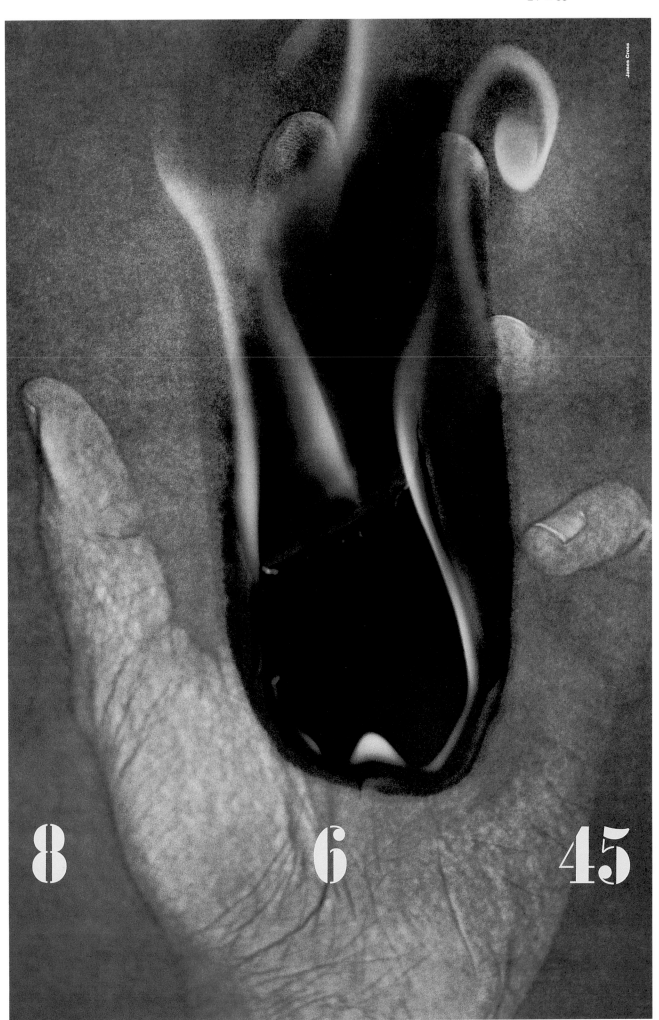

C O N N E C T I O N S

Richard Danne — "I have long been intrigued with the connection between classical music and modern jazz. I've noticed that people who love the one are usually interested in the other. Fine musicians in the classical medium enjoy the respect of jazz colleagues and vice versa. Not surprising since performing each requires commitment, sensitivity, and a high level of musicianship. The two forms often overlap and influence one another (Copland, Previn, Bernstein, the MJQ). Each can soothe or excite or extract countless other emotional responses. Classical, with European roots, and Jazz, a purely American invention, connect with audiences and generations and cultures."

Simpson
making paper
perform!

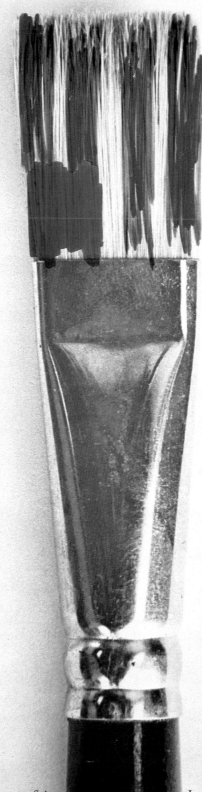

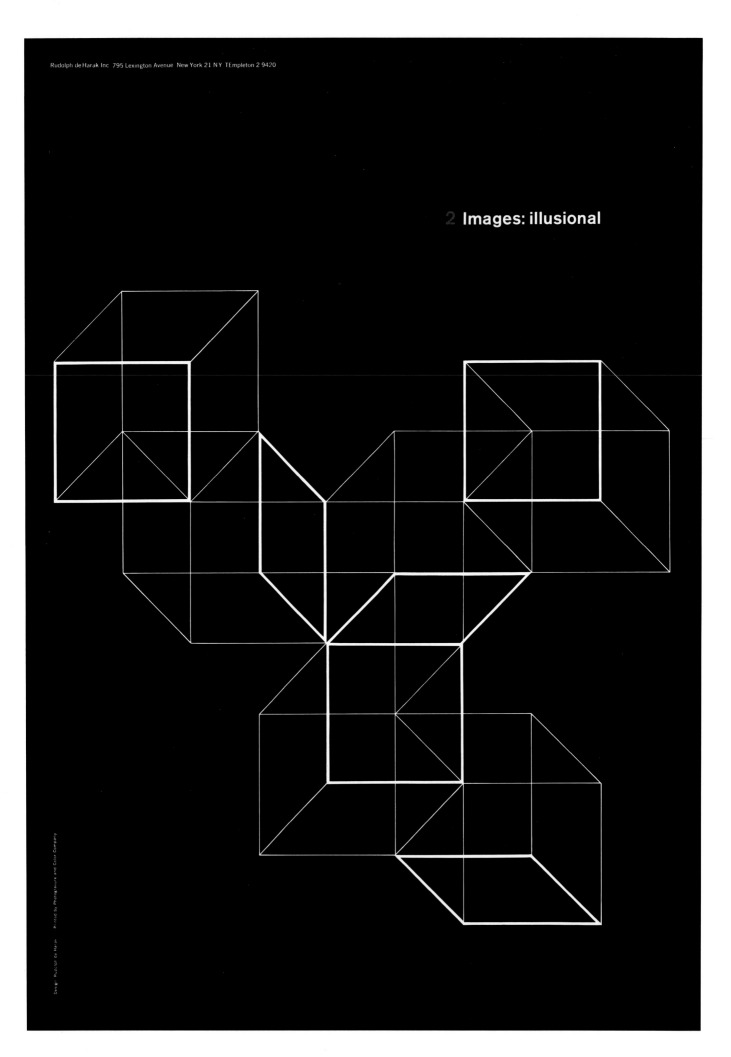

FORM & PURPOSE

The pursuit of novelty and fashion in the design of our environment is a preoccupation of our culture. Art and craft are increasingly distinct, and artists function apart from society's concern. Architects and city planners, only recently captivated by the issues of social accountability and the challenges posed by contemporary technology and bureaucracy, now retreat to narcissistic, introverted and indulgent activities—activities in which personal fascination and eclectic sophistication are the mainstays.

Ahead of us lies a world of growing numbers, dwindling resources, and limits on energy. It will require the ingenuity, inventiveness and responsiveness demonstrated in design in nature and design in indigenous cultures to achieve a balanced, affordable and wholesome environment.

The 1980 International Design Conference in Aspen will be devoted to examining *Form and Purpose*. We will search for relevant patterns and models to guide us in building an environment which will be enriching and uplifting to the human spirit.

MOSHE SAFDIE
1980 Conference Chairman

CONFERENCE FORMAT
SUNDAY EVENING
Introduction of the Speakers and IBM Fellows
Statement of the 1980 Conference Theme: Moshe Safdie
MONDAY
Design in Nature
Food, Form, and Purpose
TUESDAY
Fashionability: The Striving for Novelty
Man the Decorator: Ritual and Tradition
The Indigenous Builders
WEDNESDAY
Architecture, Form, and Purpose
Artists and Society
THURSDAY
The New Constraints: Energy and Resource
FRIDAY
Form and Purpose: Summary and Synthesis

IDCA 1980 SPEAKERS AND EVENTS:
Among the speakers at IDCA 1980 are CATHERINE BATESON, visiting scholar of anthropology at Harvard University; Architect JAMES MARSTON FITCH, professor emeritus of architectural preservation at Columbia University; STEPHEN GOULD, biologist from Harvard University, author of *Ever Since Darwin*; Neurophysiologist JERRY LETTVIN, specialist in bio-engineering from MIT; PAUL

MacCREADY, environmental engineer and designer of the man-powered flight vehicles, *The Gossamer Albatross* and *Gossamer Condor*; Architect and art historian BERNARD RUDOFSKY, author of *Architecture without Architects*; Sociologist and appropriate technology theorist ORVILLE SCHELL; OLIVER SELFRIDGE, communication systems designer and specialist in man-machine interaction; ROBERT A.M. STERN, architect and professor of architecture at Columbia University; Architect PETER STEVENS, author of *Patterns in Nature*; Coty Award-winning fashion designer, PAULINE TRIGERE.

EVENTS AT IDCA 1980 INCLUDE:
A mountaintop picnic, fashion and photography workshops, films, music, and exhibits. A special celebration of the Thirtieth Anniversary of the IDCA is planned. Upon registration, each conferee will receive a publication in which the conference theme is elaborated.

IDCA BOARD OF DIRECTORS:
Richard Farson, President;
Julian Beinart, Vice President;
Niels Diffrient, Treasurer;
Jane Thompson,
Secretary; Saul Bass;
Andrea Baynes;
Raioh;
Caplan;

Ivan Chermayeff; Lou Dorfsman; Milton Glaser; Bill Lacy; George Nelson; Jack Roberts; Frank Stanton; Jivan Tabibian; Henry Wolf.

IDCA US AND INTERNATIONAL ADVISORS:
Herbert Bayer; Peter Blake; Alf Boe; Ulla Boe; Gilles de Bure; Pat Carbine; Paul Friedberg, Leslie Julius; Wendy Keys; Kisho Kurokawa, Leo Lionni; John Massey; Elizabeth Plaepcke; Herbert Pinzke; Jaquelin Robertson; Moshe Safdie; Alex Stravske; Thomas Watson; Richard Saul Wurman.

1980 IBM FELLOWS
Theo Crosby, Architect, London; Wim Crouwel, Graphic Designer, Amsterdam; Lewis Davis, Architect, New York; Aase Eriksen, Architect, Philadelphia; Norman Foster, Architect, London; Claude Fournier, Filmmaker, Montreal; Francoise Jollant, Design Historian, Paris; Peter Kneebone, Graphic Designer, Paris; Friso Kramer, Industrial Designer, Paris; Angelo Mangarotti, Architect, Milan; Yacov Rechter, Architect, Tel Aviv; Richard Rogers,

Architect, London; Assam Salaam, Architect, London; Anand Sarabhai, Biologist, Art Patron, Ahmedabad, India; Dolf Schnebli, Architect, Zurich; Eduardo Terrazas, Architect, Mexico City; Anne Tyng, Architect, Philadelphia; Wolf Von Eckardt, Architectural Critic, Washington, D.C.

REGISTRATION
Registration is accepted from professionals and students in design and design-related fields. In the interest of conferee participation and comfort, space at IDCA 1980 will be limited. We suggest returning your application as early as possible. If we reach our limit before your application is received we may not be able to accept it and will notify you to refund your registration fee in full. No registration fees postmarked after June 5 will be accepted.

If you find it necessary to cancel your reservation, please send your refund request to IDCA. P.O. Box 664, Aspen, Colorado 81611. Attn: Registration Secretary. Requests postmarked before May 28 will be refunded at 90% of the fees paid. Requests postmarked on or after May 28 will be refunded at 80% of the fees paid.

REGISTRATION FEE Registration: (U.S. Dollars) $250. Additional Member of Household - $125; Full-time student (Proof required) - $115. List all applicants by name and make check payable to IDCA. Your canceled check is your confirmation. Government purchase orders will be honored. No food or lodging included in fee.

CONFERENCE LOCATION: Robert O. Anderson Center of the Aspen Institute for Humanistic Studies, 1000 North Third Street, Aspen, Colorado 81611.

ACCOMMODATIONS: For housing and travel information, write or telephone Nancy Erlin, c/o Aspen Ski Tours, P.O. Box 320, Aspen, Colorado 81611 (303) 925-4526. Temperature range is from 90 to 30. Bring warm clothing and casual attire.

DAILY SCHEDULE Conference schedules and literature will be distributed at the main tent on June 15, 1980 from 10 until 5. The Sunday evening program will begin at 8 p.m. The Conference will end Friday, June 20, at 12:00 noon.

CAMPING For camping information write U.S. Forest Service, 806 West Hallum, Aspen, Colorado 81611

CHILDREN'S DAY CARE For child care information write IDCA, P.O. Box 664, Aspen, Colorado 81611.

List all applicants by name and make check payable to IDCA. c/o The Bank of Aspen, P.O. Box "D", Aspen, Colorado 81611. Your canceled check is your confirmation. Government purchase orders will be honored. No food or lodging included in fees.

Design: Lou Dorfsman
Printing: Alan Lithograph, Inc.
Paper: Champion Paper Co.
ESP Retouching

JUNE 15-20, 1980

THE INTERNATIONAL DESIGN CONFERENCE IN ASPEN

THE WORLD OF

FRANKLIN&
JEFFERSON

The American Revolution Bicentennial Administration exhibition "The World of Franklin and Jefferson" was designed by the office of
Charles and Ray Eames with the cooperation of The Metropolitan Museum of Art in New York through a grant from the IBM Corporation

The Metropolitan Museum of Art
MARCH 5 through MAY 2, 1976

In a survival sense,
neither
sophisticated societies
nor
primitive tribes
have
continuity of existence assured.

Friendship and cooperation
should ease the pain.

We, the undersigned, deplore and oppose the Government's intention to introduce admission charges to national museums and galleries

(poster featuring facsimile signatures of historical figures including Caravaggio, Gainsborough, Whistler, Nicolaus Copernicus, Bruegel, Monash, A. Graham Bell, Goya, Turner, Vermeer, John Constable, James Watt, Geo. Stephenson, Rembrandt, Modigliani, Wren, A. Einstein, Tiziano Pittore, Joshua Reynolds, C.R. Darwin, Frank Lloyd Wright, and Vincent)

and Pentagram Design Partnership
—and Lund Humphries

Write in protest to your MP
and send for the petition forms to
Campaign Against Museum Admission Charges
221 Camden High Street
London NW1 7BU

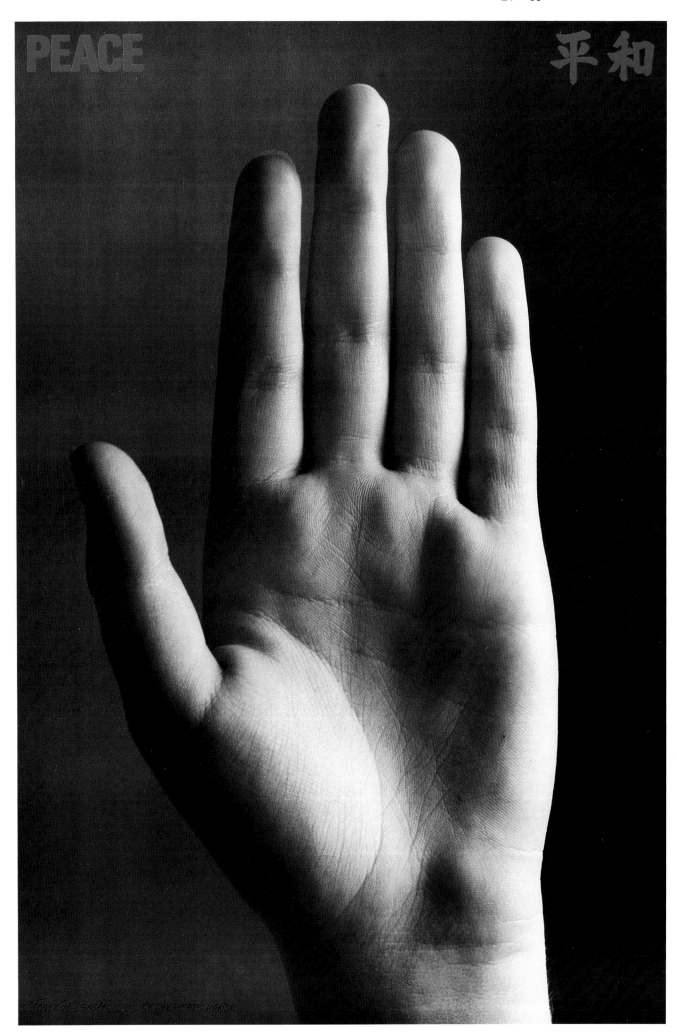

The Alvin Ailey American Dance Theater's 25th Anniversary Tour is sponsored by Philip Morris Incorporated
Design: Steff Geissbuhler, Chermayeff & Geismar Associates

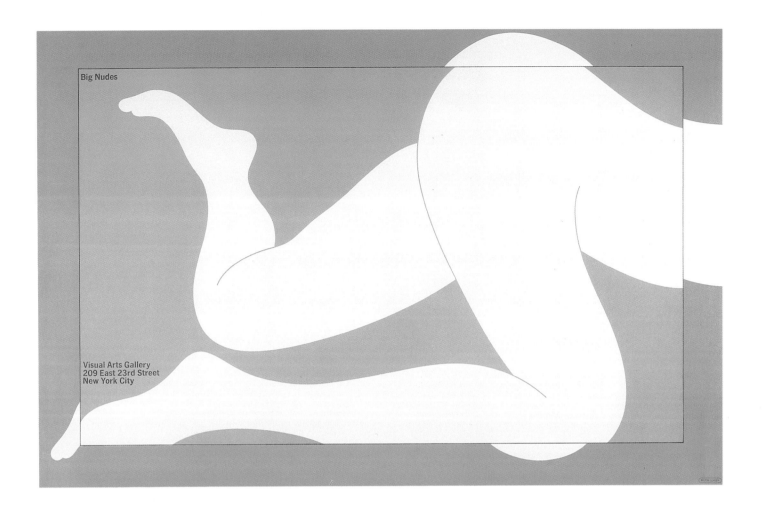

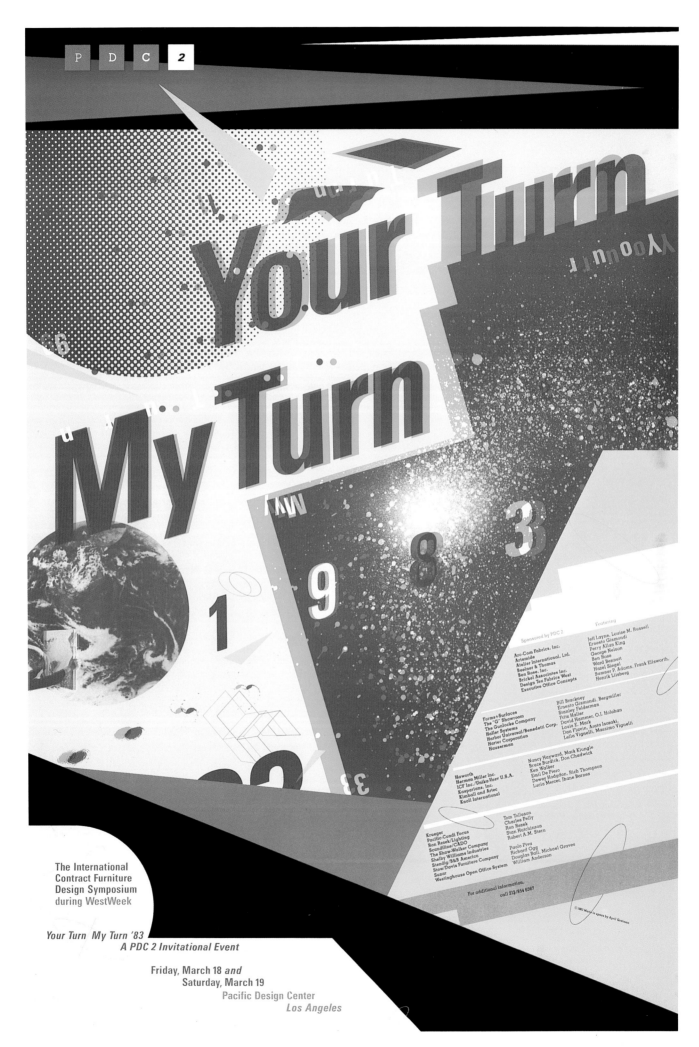

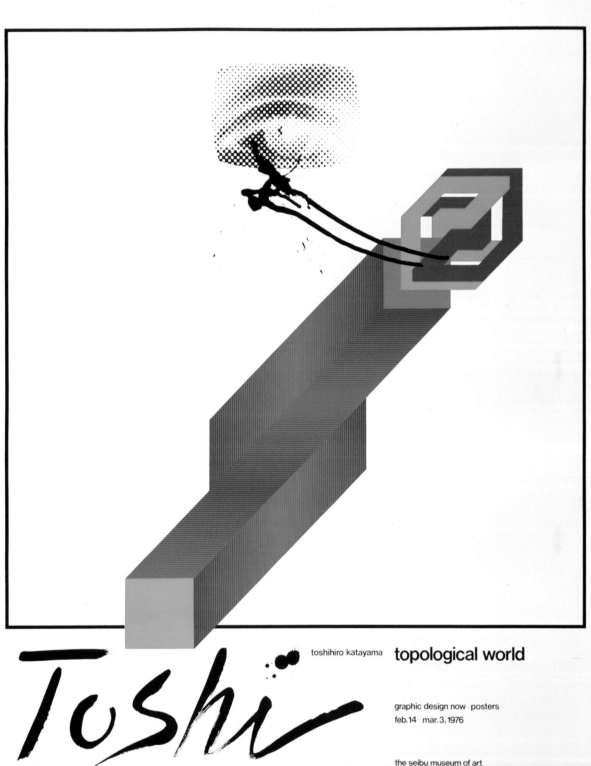

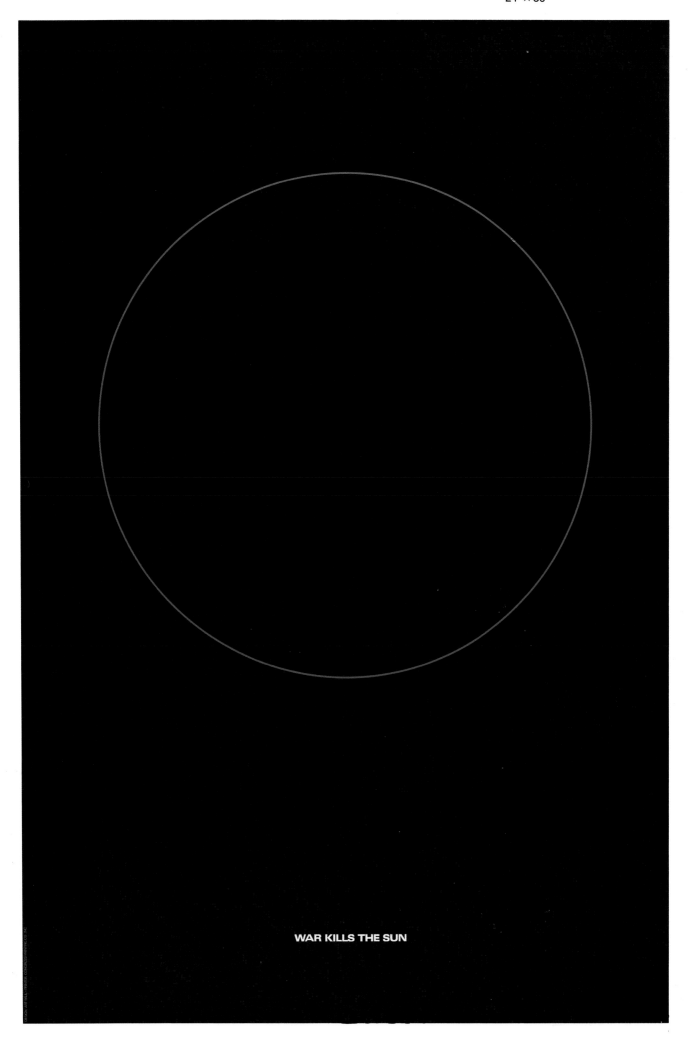

United States **Alan Peckolick** 1983 Free admission Tuesdays subsidized by Mobil Oil 30" × 46"

FREE MUSEUM OF AMERICAN FOLK ART, THE WHITNEY AND GUGGENHEIM MUSEUM TUES EVENINGS
GUGGENHEIM MUSEUM 89 ST. & FIFTH AVE. 5–8 PM
MUSEUM OF AMERICAN FOLK ART 49 WEST 53 ST. 5:30–8 PM
WHITNEY MUSEUM 75 ST. & MADISON 6–8 PM
MADE POSSIBLE BY A GRANT FROM
Mobil

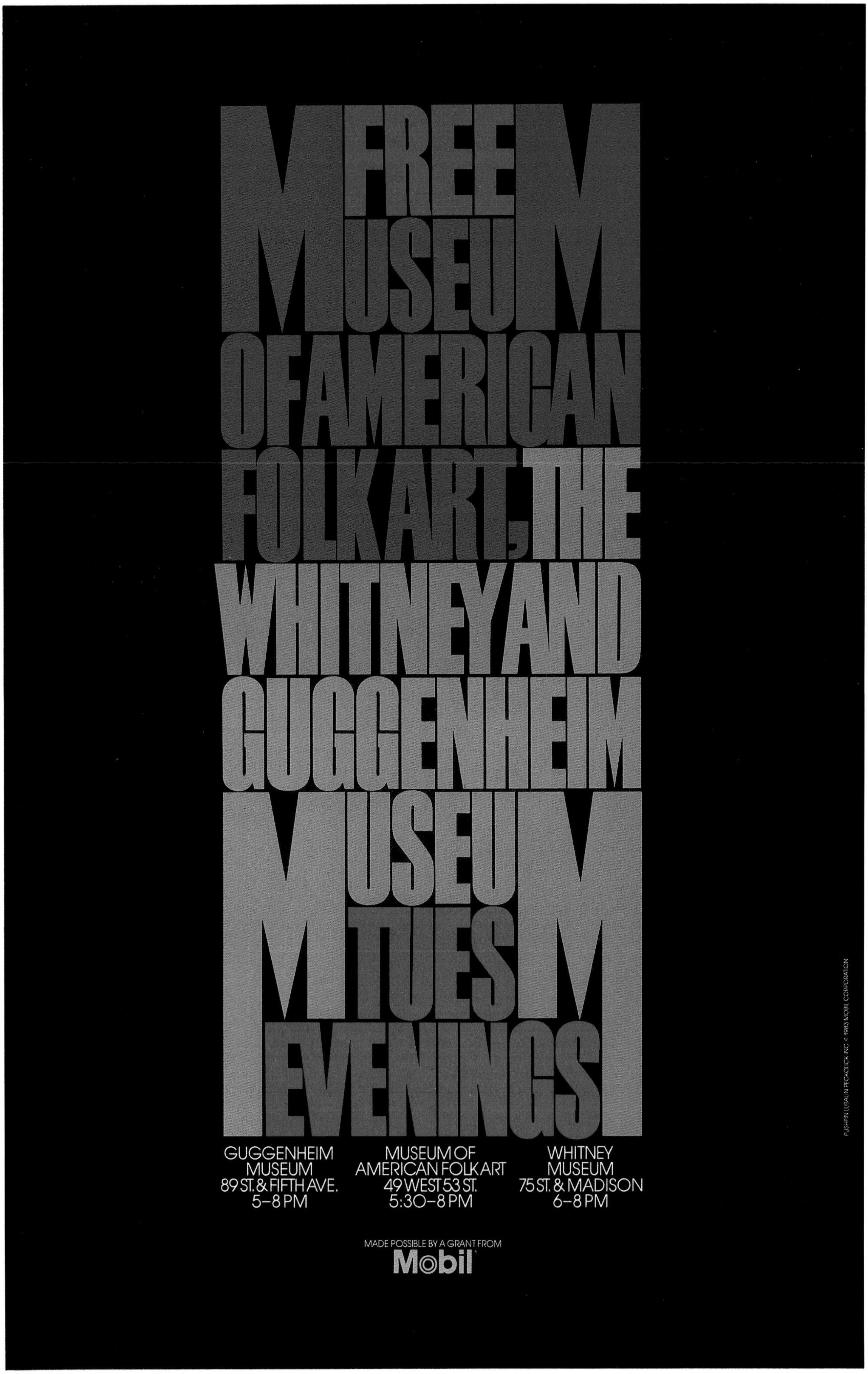

Hot Seat

Knoll International, Dallas, requests the
pleasure of your company at a special chili cookoff
commemorating the introduction of a new
collection of seating designed by Bill Stephens.
Please join us Sunday, August 22, 2–8 P.M.
If you can make it, we'll be sure to save you a seat.
R.S.V.P. 741-5819.

Paul Rand

The American Institute
of Graphic Arts
24" × 36"

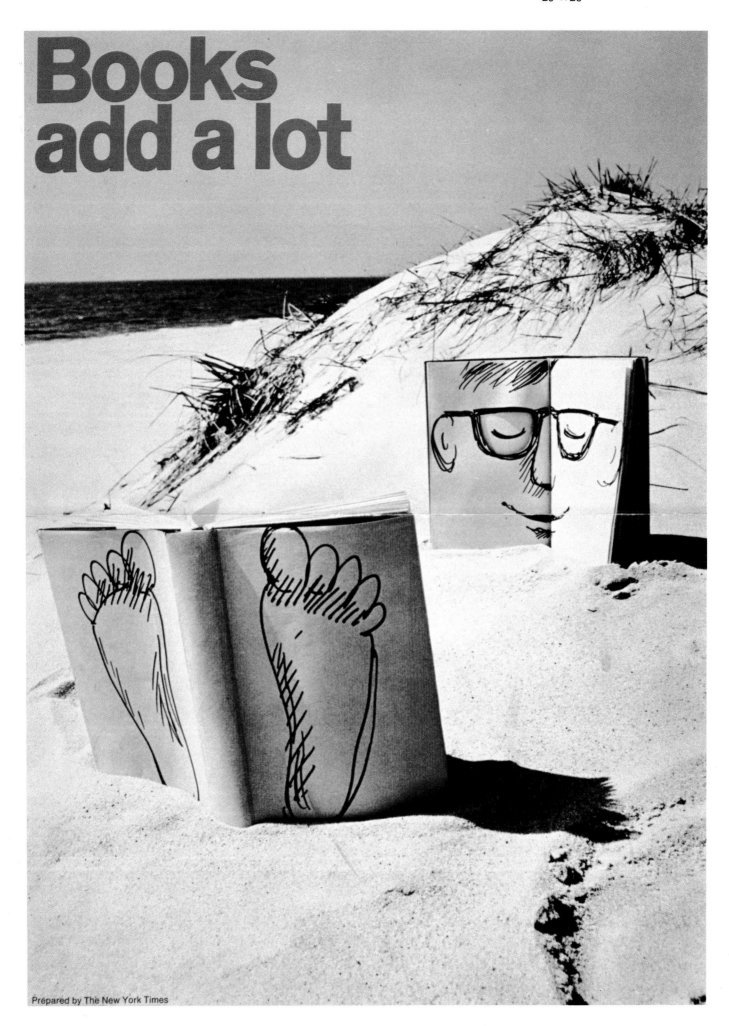

Books
add a lot

Prepared by The New York Times

Dance
20 ✱

July 9 - August 20
1967
Techniques of modern dance
Dance composition
Stagecraft for dance
Theory and methods
Dance and music
Labanotation

Faculty for the 1966 session
included Martha Graham,
José Limón, Paul Draper,
Lucas Hoving, Ruth Currier,
Betty Jones

Tickets and fees for residence
at the six-week session are $550
including a ticket to each
American Dance Festival performance.
Non-resident tuition is $325 and
includes Festival tickets

Cooperative scholarships, work opportunities,
performance scholarships,
stagecraft apprenticeships available
to a limited number of qualified applicants

For bulletin and application write to
Miss Theodora Wiesner, Director,
New London, Connecticut 06320

Connecticut College School of Dance
20th Annual Session

Bradbury Thompson
Photographs: Philip A. Biscuti
Offset: Connecticut Printers

BERLIN Art·Music·Literature·Theater·Film·Urbanism
Cultural Aspects of a City **NOW** March 12 through April 19, 1977

Sponsored by Goethe House New York   For further information call 744-8472

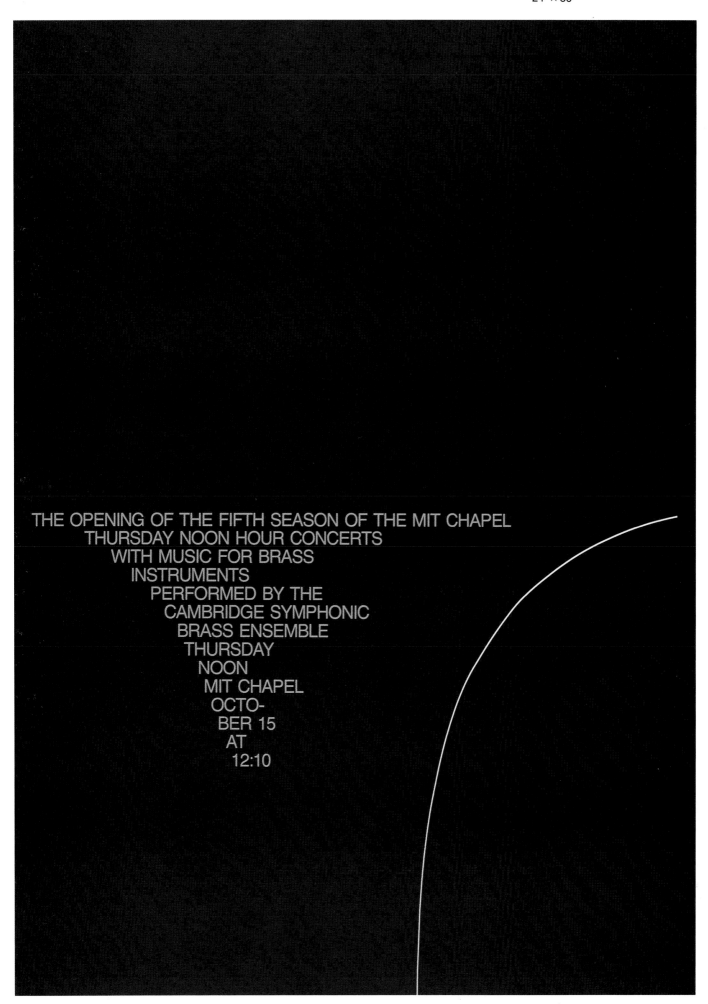

THE OPENING OF THE FIFTH SEASON OF THE MIT CHAPEL
THURSDAY NOON HOUR CONCERTS
WITH MUSIC FOR BRASS
INSTRUMENTS
PERFORMED BY THE
CAMBRIDGE SYMPHONIC
BRASS ENSEMBLE
THURSDAY
NOON
MIT CHAPEL
OCTO-
BER 15
AT
12:10

The Impact of Excellence

A symposium
in celebration
of 150 years of
photography
and design:

Peter Bunnell
Cornell Capa
Dr. Harold Edgerton
Morton Goldsholl
Allen Hurlburt
Nathan Lyons
Sidney Rapoport
Pete Turner
Henry Wolf

May 14 & 15
Rochester
Institute
of
Technology

George H. Clark
Memorial
Gymnasium
Rochester, N.Y.

Sponsored by Rochester Institute of
Technology and Eastman Kodak
Company in cooperation with
Professional Photographers of America, Inc.

Ken Cato

After studies at the Royal Melbourne Institute of Technology, Ken Cato worked in direct mailing, advertising agencies, and a design studio before forming his own company. Ken Cato Design Company Pty. Ltd. is a continuation of Cato Hibberd Design Pty. Ltd., formed in June 1970. Cato is involved primarily in packaging, corporate design, editorial design, promotional literature, architectural graphics, and signage. He is the representative for Australia on the International Advisory Board for the London College of Printing. He was named chairman of the Australian Writers' and Art Directors' Association in 1980, and was a member of the International Jury, Brno, Czechoslovakia (1978). His work has been exhibited in recent years at Brno, Leipzig, Warsaw, Lahti, and Toyama. His many awards include those of the Art Directors' Club of New York, the Australian Writers' and Art Directors' Association, and the Internationale Buchkunst-Ausstellung, Leipzig.

Les Mason

Les Mason studied at Chouinard Institute and had gained wide recognition for his work with West Coast Designers before moving to Melbourne, Australia, in 1961. He set up his own studio in South Melbourne, in 1962, becoming a major design force in packaging, corporate design, advertising, and editorial and architectural design. He relocated to Perth, Western Australia, in 1981. Mason has won many awards internationally for packaging, typography, and architectural graphics in Europe, America, Japan, and Australia. Several of his pieces were selected by an international panel as outstanding examples of twentieth-century typographic design. His work is represented in museums in Switzerland and the Art Gallery of Western Australia. He had a one-man exhibition of his paintings at Realities Gallery, Melbourne, in 1976. Mason is part-time lecturer in graphic design at Western Australia Institute of Technology.

Georg Schmid

Georg Schmid studied at the Akademie für angewandte Kunst in Vienna. Since 1950, he has worked as a freelance graphic designer, painter, and stage designer, and over the years has been lecturer at the Akademie der bildenden Künste, Vienna. He is currently involved in the design of exhibitions for various cultural institutions and museums in Austria and elsewhere. He designed the graphics for the Museum des 20. Jahrhunderts in Vienna, as well as posters and catalogues for other museums in that city. His work includes designs for the Volkstheater, Vienna, the Thalia Theater, Hamburg, programs for the Wiener Staatsoper, and stage decors and costumes for the Volkstheater and the Schauspielhaus, Zurich. Schmid was art director at Europa Verlag for many years; he now directs television films and animated films for Austrian television. His work appears in the collections of the Museum of Modern Art, New York, the National Library in Washington, the Neue Sammlung, Munich, and the Museum of Applied Arts, Vienna.

Gilles Fiszman

After a lengthy period of study at the Academy of Plastic Arts in Warsaw, Gilles Fiszman began his work as a graphic artist in Brussels in 1957. In 1962, Fiszman commenced his career as director in an advertising agency, and was named president of the Society of Belgian Graphic Designers. Fiszman specializes in poster design, trademarks, and other areas of corporate communications.

Garry Emery

Garry Emery, whose design practice is located in Melbourne, Australia, is engaged in a broad range of graphic communications including visual identity programs, promotion and advertising, corporate communications, and architectural and environmental graphics. He has recently been appointed graphics consultant for the new parliament house in Canberra and the Australian embassy in Beijing in the People's Republic of China. He is concurrently involved in design education.

Barrie Tucker

Barrie Tucker began his career in Australia, working in advertising before traveling to Europe in 1966. He worked as a designer and art director in Switzerland and freelanced as an illustrator/designer in London before returning to Australia in 1970. In 1972, Tucker started his own design consultancy in Adelaide, producing award-winning designs for numerous national clients. He became the first Australian to have work selected and exhibited in the New York Art Directors' Show and featured on the cover of *Graphis* magazine. His work has appeared in numerous international publications, including *Communication Arts*, *Publicité*, and *Advertising Art*. Tucker's work has received recognition at the Swiss National Poster Exhibition, New York Art Directors' Club Awards shows, and the Brno Biennale. He is guest lecturer at South Australian College of Design, and Associate of the Industrial Design Institute of Australia and the Industrial Design Council of Australia.

Jacques Richez

Jacques Richez, largely self-taught freelance designer, received his formal art training at the Académie Royale des Beaux-Arts in Mons, before joining a design studio in Brussels. On his return from World War II, he set up his own practice, working on advertising projects and posters. He designed the official poster and booklet, *Bâtir le monde pour l'homme,* for the 1958 Brussels World Fair. In 1969, Richez was in charge of the overall design concept for the Kinshasa International Fair, and the following year designed two mural panels 65 meters square for the Belgian pavilion at Expo '70 in Osaka. He was chosen by *Photography Year 1973* as one of the forty most original artists in the field of experimental photography. He is the author of *Marques, signes et symboles* (Brussels, 1972), and *Textes et prétextes, 35 ans de réflexion(s) sur le graphisme* (Brussels, 1980).

Stuart B. Ash

Stuart B. Ash studied graphic design at Western Technical School from 1957 to 1962, and at Ontario College of Art from 1962 to 1964, where he taught advanced typography in 1979. After working for Cooper and Beatty and for Paul Arthur Associates, he entered into partnership with Fritz Gottschalk. Gottschalk + Ash International have established offices in Montreal, Toronto, New York, and Zurich. Each office provides a total service and operates independently, yet still offers the opportunity to exchange business and design experience over a broader base, unified by a shared dedication and commitment to design. Exhibitions were held in Mead Library of Ideas in New York in 1967, at the National Gallery of Canada in 1969, at the Museum of Fine Arts in Montreal in 1970, and in the Swiss graphics exhibition at the Louvre in 1971. Ash has received many national and international awards.

Theo Dimson

Theo Dimson graduated with honors in graphic design from the Ontario College of Art, Toronto, in 1950. He began his career at Art Associates Limited, and became their vice-president and creative director in 1960. In 1965, he established his own design firm. His work has been exhibited in all major international graphic-design exhibitions and has won numerous awards, best-of-shows, and gold and silver medals. His works have been exhibited and published in Canada, the United States, England, France, Bulgaria, Poland, Finland, and Japan. Dimson was the first winner of the Usherwood Award for continuous outstanding contribution to the visual arts in Canada. He is author of *Great Canadian Posters,* published by Oxford University Press. His posters are in the collections of the Public Archives, Ottawa, and in private collections internationally. He is a member of the Royal Canadian Academy of Arts, the Ontario College of Art, the Society of Graphic Designers of Canada, and the Art Directors' Club, Toronto.

Burton Kramer

Burton Kramer established his design consulting office in Toronto in 1967 after working in New York and Zurich. He is a graduate of Yale University, the Chicago Institute of Design, and was a Fulbright Scholar at the Royal College of Art, London. Kramer has been a member of the graphic design faculty of the Ontario College of Art since 1978. Best known for his symbol and visual identity program for the CBC, Kramer is involved in a wide range of work encompassing corporate identity, environmental-architectural graphics, exhibitions, publications, posters, packaging, and three-dimensional graphics. Recipient of numerous national and international awards, he has lectured at colleges and universities, and exhibited his work throughout the world. His work is included in many major international collections, publications, and annuals. He has designed two important Canadian art books, *The Art of Norval Morrisseau* in 1979, and *Passionate Spirits* in 1980.

Ernst Roch

Ernst Roch studied graphic design at the Staatliche Meisterschule für angewandte Kunst in Graz from 1948 to 1953. After immigration to Canada in 1953, he was employed first as a designer then design director in various studios. He opened his own design office in 1960 and in 1965 co-founded Design Collaborative. Since 1977, he heads Roch Design, the graphic, environmental design firm. He has undertaken a wide range of individual design projects, including trademarks, posters, packaging, books, postage stamps, corporate, security, and architectural graphics, as well as complete visual identity programs. The recipient of numerous awards, Roch is represented in the collections of the National Archives, Ottawa, the Library of Congress, Washington, D.C., the Museum of Modern Art, New York, and the International Poster Museum, Warsaw. He is a member of the Royal Canadian Academy of Arts, the American Institute of Graphic Arts, and a fellow of the Association of Graphic Designers of Canada.

Heather Cooper

Heather Cooper began her career as an apprentice in a design studio at the age of eighteen. In 1968, after five years as a staff designer, she began an illustration and design practice in Toronto. Her collaboration with Robert Burns in 1970 led to the partnership of Burns and Cooper, which later became Burns, Cooper, Hynes Limited. In January 1984, as a result of diverging interests, Cooper formed her own company. Her talent and success as an illustrator are matched by her equally notable accomplishments as a designer. A retrospective exhibition of her work entitled "The Art of the Illustrator" was staged in Toronto in 1975. Cooper has received the gold medals of both the New York Society of Illustrators and the New York Art Directors' Club, a bronze medal from the Brno Biennale, and numerous other awards from Graphica, the Toronto Art Directors' Club, CA, and Creativity. Cooper is a member of the Royal Canadian Academy.

Rolf Harder

Rolf Harder, now a Canadian citizen, studied at the Hamburg Academy of Fine Arts from 1948 to 1952. He worked as a designer and art director in German and Canadian studios and agencies until 1959 when he set up his own design office in Montreal. A founding partner of Design Collaborative (1965–1977), since 1977 he has headed Rolf Harder & Associates, Inc. Harder's work was featured, together with that of Ernst Roch, in a government-sponsored traveling exhibition shown throughout Canada, in the United States, and in Europe. He was one of two Canadian representatives in the experimental graphics section at the 36th Venice Biennale. He is represented in many national and international exhibitions and publications, and has lectured throughout Canada. Harder is a member of the Royal Canadian Academy of Arts, the American Institute of Graphic Arts, and a fellow of the Society of Graphic Designers of Canada.

Jean Morin

Jean Morin graduated from the Ecole des Beaux-Arts in Quebec City in 1960 and did post-graduate work at the Kunstgewerbeschule in Zurich. He started his career as a graphic designer in 1961, working successively for the Canadian Government Exhibition Commission, Fritz Seigner, Ernst Roch, James Valkus Inc., Gagnon/Valkus Inc., and Girard Bruce and Associates. Morin has been a design consultant since 1968 and is a partner in the firm of Morin, Lessard, McInnis Inc. with offices in Montreal and Toronto. Morin specializes in corporate visual identity programs, packaging, signage, and postage stamps. He is a lecturer at leading design schools and serves on the juries of graphic design competitions. Morin is a laureate of Industrial Graphic International and of the American Institute of Graphic Arts.

Josef Flejsar
Joseph Flejsar studied at the Academy of Applied Art in Prague. Beginning as a freelance artist in book design and exhibition display in 1946, he subsequently widened his scope to include advertising. Between 1960 and 1979, he organized numerous exhibitions of poster and folk art in various countries, and since 1969 has been artistic consultant to the House of Czechoslovak Children in Prague Castle, for which he has created murals and tapestries. His work has appeared in one-man shows in Prague, Helsinki, and at Southern Connecticut State College in New Haven. Examples of his work have also been exhibited in Austria, Hungary, Switzerland, Japan, West Germany, Poland, England, and Italy. He was awarded gold and silver medals for design at the International Jewelry Exhibition, Jablonec, in 1965 and 1968, and critics' prize for posters at the Brno Biennale; he was also named laureate of the Warsaw Biennale in 1970.

Vladislav Rostoka
Vladislav Rostoka has been living and working in Bratislava as a freelance graphic designer. His design work includes posters, trademarks and symbols, and corporate identity programs as well as covers, typographic layouts, and illustrations for studios, agencies, and publishing houses. His graphic designs have been shown in eight one-man exhibitions and his work has appeared at more than one hundred collective exhibitions in Czechoslovakia and abroad. He is a regular participant in the international exhibitions at Brno, Warsaw, Lahti, and Colorado. A prize winner in the Brno Biennale in 1982, and the Lahti Biennale in 1985, he has received frequent recognition in the Best Books of the Year competition in Czechoslovakia. Rostoka's work is represented in the collections of the Moravian Gallery, Brno, the Applied Arts Museum, Prague, the National Gallery, Bratislava, the National Museum, Warsaw, the City Museum, Lahti, and the National Library, Zagreb. He is a member of the Union of Slovak Creative Artists.

Zdenek Ziegler
After studies in the department of architecture at Czech Technical University, Prague, Zdenek Ziegler began to work as a freelance designer. His range of design projects includes posters, trademarks and symbols, books, and exhibition and interior design. A current contributor to the international exhibitions in Warsaw, Brno, Lahti, Toyama, and Denver, his posters, books, and graphics have been shown in one-man exhibitions in Prague, Frankfurt, Stuttgart, and Chob. Ziegler has received numerous awards and distinctions in Czechoslovakia and abroad. He sits on the jury of various competitions and his works are represented in the collections of the Museum of Modern Art, New York, and the Stedelijk Museum. He is a member of the Association of Czech Creative Artists.

Flemming Ljorring
Flemming Ljorring trained as a lithographic artist in Copenhagen from 1956 to 1960. He worked as a layout artist with Allhems Forlag AB in Sweden, then studied creative design at Den Grafiske Hojskole in Copenhagen. Subsequently art director at Fritz Schur AS Printing Company, Ljorring opened his own studio in 1964, specializing in graphic design, photography, book design, and typography. Ljorring was appointed jury member for the Danish Retail Hardware Association in 1973, the international poster competition "La Prévention Routière" in Paris in 1974, the poster competition for Bertolt Brecht's eightieth birthday in East Berlin, and the honorary committees of the 8th Brno Biennale and the 7th Warsaw Biennale. A participant in the American Institute of Graphic Arts group exhibition "Color" at the Whitney Museum in New York in 1974, Ljorring was speaker at the International Design Conference in Aspen in 1978, and member of the program committee at the 1978 Chicago Congress "Design That Works."

Jan Rajlich
Jan Rajlich received his art training at Skola eumni at Zlin, from 1939 to 1945. Since 1950, he has been living and working as a painter and graphic designer in Brno. Having focused his interest on graphic design without relinquishing free art, he has designed a great number of posters, signs, and symbols as well as typographic layouts for numerous publications. His paintings, drawings, and applied graphics have been exhibited in twenty-two one-man shows, and his posters especially have been shown at more than sixty collective exhibitions in Czechoslovakia and an equal number of venues abroad. His work is represented in the collections of the Museum of Modern Art, New York, the Muzeum Plakata, Warsaw, the Neue Sammlung, Munich, and in many other museums and private collections. Rajlich was an award winner at the 1st and 10th Biennale at Brno. A member of the Association of Czech Creative Artists, he is the founder of the Brno Biennale of Graphic Design, and its president since its inception.

Jaroslav Sura
Jaroslav Sura studied in Prague from 1948 to 1954 under Professor Karel Svolinsky at the Academy of Fine Arts. He then set up as a freelance artist, collaborating with his wife, graphic artist Vera Surová. His field is nonfigurative and decorative painting, graphic art, illustration, and poster design. Sura's work, which has been exhibited internationally, is represented in public and private collections worldwide. Sura was awarded first prize at the Festival of Czechoslovak Art in Prague in 1959, first prize in Helsinki in 1962, first prize for graphic art at the 12th Mostra G. Santelli in Florence in 1972, first prize in competition at Brno in 1976, Most Beautiful Czechoslovakian Book competition prize in 1976, and the special prize at the 10th Biennale in Warsaw in 1984. Sura is a member of the Association of Czech Creative Artists.

Martti Mykkänen

Martti Mykkänen completed training at Helsinki School of Arts and Crafts in 1951, then studied in Switzerland. He was illustrator for the magazine *Uusi Kuvalehti* from 1953 to 1954, subsequently setting up a freelance practice working for government ministries and publishers, and designing posters for several presidential election campaigns. Mykkänen is a contributor to *Look at Finland,* published by the Ministry of Foreign Affairs and Finnish Tourist Board and *YV,* a monthly magazine of the Central Bank of Cooperative Banks, Helsinki. A participant in many international exhibitions between 1966 and 1968, he was president of the international jury at the Warsaw Biennale in 1972. Mykkänen received a gold medal at the Catania 5th International Poster Exhibition in Italy in 1971, and the Goldene Reisekutsche at the Darmstadt International Tourist Poster Competition in 1973. Mykkänen has lectured on book-jacket design for Finnish television. His works are represented in the collections of the Royal Ontario Museum, Toronto, and the Stedelijk Museum.

Jean Carlu

Jean Carlu, after a period of training as an architect, turned in 1918 to the field of graphic art and exhibition design. He is with Cassandre one of the pioneers of modern poster art and belonged to the small group of artists whose new visual expression revolutionized this field of graphic art after 1924. He served in 1937 as chairman of Graphic Publicity Section of the Paris International Exhibition. In 1940, he was sent by the French Government on a mission to the United States, remained for the next thirteen years. Carlu worked for the Office of War Information and various groups of La France Libre, and in 1941 produced the first U.S. Defense poster which received a medal from the Art Directors' Club of New York. Between 1945 and 1955, simultaneously with his work for American firms, he was commissioned by the French Government to plan educational and commerical exhibitions in the United States. In 1953, he returned to France where he continued to design posters and acted as consultant art director for various companies.

Jacques Dubois

Jacques Dubois studied at the Ecole Nationale des Arts Décoratifs in Paris under Jean Carlu and poster designer A. M. Cassandre. He contributed to the Pavilion of Advertising at the 1937 Arts et Techniques Exhibition in Paris, winning a diplôme d'honneur. Until World War II, he was mainly concerned with photography, and was commissioned as a photo reporter in North Africa for a shipping company periodical. In 1943, he began to design tapestry cartoons for Feltin and worked on theater decor. From 1946 to 1968, he worked on publicity for the French National Tourist Office, producing advertising materials for firms including Vittel, Pathé-Marconi, Longines, Air France, Larousse, Crédit Lyonnais, and Van Cleef and Arpels. His brochure for the third centenary of the Saint-Gobain company won international first prize for advertising photography at the 1966 Communications Fair in Genoa. His work is represented in the collections of the Museum of Modern Art, Paris.

Marcel Jacno

Marcel Jacno is self-taught as an artist. Until 1931, he did animated cartoons and cinema posters, then began designing typefaces, including *Jacno* (1948) for Fonderies Deberny at Peignot, Paris, *Chaillot* (1951) for the Théâtre National Populaire, *Molière* (1971) for the Comédie Française, and *Ménilmontant* (1973) for the Théâtre de l'Est Parisien. Jacno has designed posters for these and all the national theaters, and packaging for Courvoisier brandy and Guerlain perfume. The Gauloises package of the French Tobacco Administration, among the most familiar objects in daily use, was designed by Jacno. He taught at the School of Fine and Applied Arts in New York in 1937, and at various art schools in Paris (1936, 1960–1961). While in the United States, Jacno illustrated publications for Hiram Walker Whisky. His many awards include the 1968 Oscar de la publicité for the entirety of his graphic work. A retrospective exhibition of his work was held in Milan in 1981.

Jukka Veistola

Jukka Veistola was awarded a scholarship to study at Ateneum Art School, Helsinki, in 1966. After completing training in 1968, he began to work in a variety of media including film, cartoon illustration, and photography. He has been a member of the board of directors of Finnish Sales and Advertising Association, of Mainosgraafikot, and of Grafia. Veistola's posters have gained numerous awards, including first prize in UNICEF competition in 1969, first and third prizes at Warsaw in 1970, and first prize in the European Outdoor Poster Competition in London in 1972. Recipient of Best Poster of the Year and Best Advertising of the Year awards, in 1971 he was awarded the Finnish Industrial Art Prize for outstanding work in graphics.

Roman Cieslewicz

Roman Cieslewicz graduated from Cracow Academy of Arts in 1955. He worked for WAG agency in Warsaw and until 1962 was art director for the magazine *Ty i Ja.* He moved to Paris in 1963, where he worked for *Vogue* and *Elle,* and created the graphic images of *Opus International, Musique en eux, Kitsch,* and *Cnac-archives.* French citizen since 1971, Cieslewicz taught at the Ecole Nationale Supérieure des Arts Graphiques from 1972 to 1975, and since 1975 teaches at the Ecole Supérieure des Arts Graphiques in Paris. Designer of books and book jackets, Cieslewicz designed new visual formulars for the magazines *20 siècle* and *Kamikaze.* Cieslewicz has designed catalogues for art institutions including the Georges Pompidou Center. His work was exhibited at the Musée des Arts Décoratifs in Paris in 1972, the Stedelijk Museum in 1973, and the Venice Biennale in 1976. Having designed some four hundred posters since 1955, Cieslewicz received two Grand Prix for film posters in Czechoslovakia in 1964 and at Warsaw in 1972, and a special prize for film posters at Cannes in 1973.

Jacques N. Garamond

Jacques Garamond studied at the Ecole Nationale Supérieure des Arts Décoratifs in Paris. He has worked as a graphic artist and artistic adviser with various commercial organizations and cultural institutions, including UNESCO, Air France, and the Office Technique pour l'Utilisation de l'Acier. Garamond has produced a large body of work that includes book design, posters, company logotypes and trademarks, and illustrations. His works have been exhibited at the important international exhibitions in Paris, Brussels, Milan, New York, Toronto, Turin, and Amsterdam. Formerly Professor of Graphics and Design at the Ecole Nationale Supérieure des Arts Décoratifs and at the Ecole Supérieure des Arts Graphiques, Garamond is founder-member of the Alliance Graphique Internationale.

Jean Widmer

Jean Widmer studied at the Kunstgewerbeschule, Zurich, and the Ecole des Beaux-Arts, Paris. From 1955 to 1959, he was art director at SNIP advertising agency and then for three years at Galeries Lafayette department store. From 1961 to 1970, he was art director for the magazine *Jardin des Modes;* he subsequently set up his own design studio. Widmer designs posters and publicity material for various museums and exhibition centers. He was in charge of the corporate identity program, and sign and information systems at the Georges Pompidou Center; he has also designed sign systems for the Louvre Museum (1980), the Musée du Château de Versailles (1980), and the Musée d'Orsay (1983). He is responsible for the design of the first touristic sign system for French highways. Widmer teaches at the Ecole Nationale Supérieure des Arts Décoratifs in Paris.

Karl Oskar Blase
Karl Oskar Blase studied applied art at the Werkkunstschule in Wuppertal from 1945 to 1949. In 1950, he set up the Müller-Blase studio with Felix Müller in Wuppertal. In 1952, he became director of Amerika-Haus graphic arts studio in Bonn. In 1958, Blase taught at the Staatliche Werkkunstschule in Kassel, co-founding the Novum group in the same year. In 1966, he was appointed professor at the Gesamthochschule in Kassel, and was co-organizer of the international exhibition Documenta in that city in 1964, 1968, 1972, and 1977. Besides poster work and exhibition planning and display, Blase specializes in postage stamp design, for which he has won many awards. Blase was a contributor to the periodical *form* from 1957 to 1966. His work has been shown on both sides of the Atlantic, in South Africa, India, and Japan. He was seven-time winner of the Best Poster of the Year award between 1956 and 1966. Examples of his work have been acquired by museums in Amsterdam, Berkeley, Cleveland, Bonn, and by several private German collectors.

Frieder Grindler
Frieder Grindler received his design training under Hans Hillmann in Kassel. From 1966 to 1979, he was art director with Süddeutschen Rundfunk in Stuttgart, with some forty film and video programs to his credit. Since 1966, he has concentrated on theater posters and record-cover design. He currently teaches design in Würzburg. His works, which have appeared widely, are represented in museums and private collections. Grindler was awarded first prize at the Finnish Poster Biennale (1981), and a gold medal at Warsaw (1984).

Hans-Peter Hoch
Hans-Peter Hoch received his professional education at the Höhere Fachschule für Grafische Gewerbe in Stuttgart in 1946, at the Arbeitsgemeinschaft bildende Künstler in Bernstein from 1946 to 1949, and at the Akademie für bildende Künste in Stuttgart from 1949 to 1951. He runs a studio for visual communication and graphic design. At the beginning, he worked for the investment industry. In recent years, he has specialized in corporate design identity programs and signage systems. He is also occupied with total visualization and the design of themes of art, culture, and technique for exhibitions and museums. In 1973, he was responsible for organizing the Kieler Woche competition. He has gained several awards for the best poster and a special prize at the 7th Competition for Graphic Design in West Germany in 1981.

Günther Kieser
Günther Kieser studied from 1947 to 1950 at the Werkkunstschule in Offenbach. From 1952 to 1964, he had a joint studio for graphic design with Hans Michel. Since then he has worked continuously as a freelance designer in many fields, including collaboration with the Lippmann & Rau and R. Schulte Bahrenberg concert agencies, the furniture firm Zapp, Fischer Verlag, and the Hessischer Rundfunk. He has designed exhibitions, and an information system for Bank für Gemeinwirtschaft, Frankfurt. He had a one-man show at Lincoln Center in New York in 1972, and has participated in many international exhibitions. In 1966, he received an award from the Art Directors' Club of New York, and a gold medal at an East European exhibition in 1968. Kieser's works are represented in the Museum of Modern Art, New York, and other collections.

Heinz Edelmann
Educated at the Kunstakademie, Düsseldorf, from 1953 to 1958, Heinz Edelmann has lived, worked, and taught in Düsseldorf, Cologne, and the Hague. For the past few years, he has concentrated on book and book-jacket design, and advertising design; he has also done some magazine illustrations. Edelmann currently lives and teaches in Düsseldorf.

Hans Hillmann
Hans Hillmann studied from 1948 to 1953 in Kassel and traveled for further study in Southern Italy. He began freelance graphic design in Kassel in 1953, specializing in film posters which remained one of his main activities until 1974. Seeing himself primarily as an illustrator, Hillmann has worked for *Twen, Der Stern, Transatlantik, Süddeutsche Zeitung,* and *Frankfurter Allgemeine Magazin.* He has been professor at the Hochschule für bildende Künste in Kassel since 1961. Hillmann was a contributor to Documenta III in 1964, to the Warsaw International Poster Biennale between 1966 and 1972, and to the Experimental Graphic Design exhibition at the Venice Biennale in 1972. His awards include first prize at the Cinema Sixteen Society, Colombo, and honorary mention at the 1st International Film Festival, Paris, 1975. His picture book *Fly Paper* is based on a story by Hammett.

Herbert W. Kapitzki
Herbert W. Kapitzki studied in Danzig, then in Hamburg and Bernstein, before attending the Staatliche Akademie der bildenden Künste in Stuttgart from 1948 to 1952. Self-taught in graphic art, he became freelance in the field of visual communication in 1953. In 1956, Kapitzki began work for the Landesgewerbeamt and the Ministry of Economic Affairs of Baden-Wurttemberg, at which time he began a scientific inquiry into the theory and practice of design in mass media. Appointed department head at the Hochschule for Gestaltung, Ulm, in 1964, in 1969 he became head of the Institute of Visual Communication at Frankfurt, a branch of the newly founded Institute of Environmental Design. He moved to Berlin in 1970 as professor of visual communication at the State Academy of Fine Arts. In 1971, Kapitzki was charged with redesigning the Historical Museum in Frankfurt. He has designed numerous exhibitions, including his work for the German contribution to the Montreal Expo in 1967.

Pierre Mendell
Pierre Mendell studied graphic design at the Kunstgewerbeschule in Basel with Armin Hofmann. He worked together with Michael Engelman in Munich in 1960, and established his own design studio in cooperation with Klaus Oberer in the Bavarian capital in 1961. His graphic concept distinguishes itself through direct visual appeal, omitting short-lived and fashionable trends. Mendell received the gold medal of the Art Directors' Club in 1973. His work has been acquired by the Museum of Modern Art, New York, and the Stedelijk Museum.

Isolde Monson-Baumgart
Isolde Monson-Baumgart studied graphic design with Hans Leistikow and Hans Hillmann at the Kassel Hochschule. While still a student, she received commissions for film posters and established a reputation from awards for her work in national and international shows. In 1959, she went to Paris to study engraving and color printmaking with S. W. Hayter. She worked as a freelance graphic designer and printmaker in Frankfurt and Paris, with emphasis on poster and postage stamp design and magazine illustration. In 1976, she moved to the United States, settling in New England. In 1980, she was guest professor in Nairobi, Kenya, for a workshop on book design. She taught at the University of Connecticut (1980–1984), and in 1984 was named chairperson at the Merz Akademie in Stuttgart. She is represented in the collections of the Bibliothèque Nationale, Paris, the national galleries of Stuttgart and Oslo, the State Library in Berlin, and other museums in Europe and throughout the United States.

Gunter Rambow
Gunter Rambow, who was trained as a glass painter, studied at the Hochschule für bildende Künste in Kassel until 1964. Together with Gerhard Lienemeyer, he founded a design studio in 1960. In 1967, the Kohlkunstverlag was founded, and one year later Michael van de Sand, who studied at the Fachhochschule Niederrhein in Krefeld, joined the team. He became partner of the studio in 1973. The team specialized in theater, literature, and other posters. They carry everyday reality—in newsy black-and-white—into the theatrical context, telling a story that is compounded of the specific city world and the theater world. The team has participated in many national and international group shows since 1961. Awards include first prize at a poster exhibition at Colorado State University in 1979, first prize and gold medal at Warsaw (1980), and silver and bronze medals at Essen in 1981.

Anton Stankowski
After serving an apprenticeship as a decorator, Anton Stankowski studied art under Max Burchartz at the Folkwangschule in Essen. From 1929 to 1937, he worked as a commercial artist in Zurich. He set up his own design office in Stuttgart in 1937. Visiting lecturer on visual communication at the Hochschule für Gestaltung, Ulm (1964), Stankowski was elected president of the German section of the Alliance Graphique Internationale in 1972, and was chairman of the visual aids commission for the Munich Olympic Games. In 1976, he received an honorary professorship from Baden-Württemberg. Stankowski had a one-man exhibition at Goethe House in New York in 1975, and has received numerous awards for his graphic design and painting. Stankowski specializes in the design of corporate symbols. Examples of his work have been acquired by museums in Europe and abroad.

Mel Calman
Mel Calman trained in London at Saint Martin's School of Art and Goldsmith's College. In 1957, he joined the *Daily Express* as a cartoonist. From 1963 to 1964, Calman worked as a cartoonist for the British Broadcasting Corporation, for the *Sunday Telegraph,* and the *Observer.* Cartoonist with the *Sunday Times* since 1965, his work is characterized by humor and economy. Calman conveys his ideas with simplicity and directness, while interest in verbal and visual communication emerges from his activities as writer and journalist. His feature *Men and Women* is syndicated in America.

Rolf Müller
Rolf Müller studied at the Hochschule für Gestaltung in Ulm and apprenticed with Josef Müller-Brockmann. He has run his own design office since 1965. From 1967 to 1972, Müller worked with Otl Aicher and served as deputy representative for the design of the Games of the 20th Olympiad in Munich in 1972. Müller designs information and signage systems for exhibitions and architectural complexes for clients including the University of Regensburg and the municipality of Bonn. He has taught at the Kunstgewerbeschule, Zurich, and other design schools. A one-man exhibition on corporate design and typography traveled through Germany in 1985. His posters are represented in Warsaw, New York, Munich, and Zurich collections. Müller is editor of *HQ: High Quality* magazine.

Helmut Schmidt-Rhen
Before studying art painting and graphic design at the Kunstakademie, Kassel, Helmut Schmidt-Rhen worked as a bookseller. From 1961 to 1965, he was art director for GGK in Switzerland. He was art director of the business magazine *Capital* (1967–1968), and was lecturer at Werkkunstschule, Düsseldorf, from 1968 to 1973. Since 1976, he has been Professor of Design at the Fachhochschule, Düsseldorf. Recipient of national and international awards, Schmidt-Rhen is a member of the Deutscher Werkbund.

Bruno K. Wiese
Bruno K. Wiese studied from 1945 to 1949 at the Staatliche Hochschule für bildende Künste in Berlin, chiefly in the tectonics class under Professor O. H. W. Hadank. Subsequently employed in Hadank's studio in Hamburg, Wiese founded his own studio for visual design in 1945. Design consultant in industry and for various institutions, he has served as expert and examiner for, among others, the city authorities for art and science in Hamburg. Visiting lecturer at the Special College of Design in Hamburg (1977–1978), he was lecturer in communication design, Fachhochschule, Kiel (1978), before being named professor there in 1981. Recipient of many prizes and awards, Wiese won first prize in the International Industrial Design Society of America Award Competition in 1983.

Margaret Calvert
After studying illustration in London at the Chelsea School of Art from 1954 to 1958, Margaret Calvert was invited to join Jock Kinneir as assistant. In 1964, she became partner in Kinneir Calvert and Associates, and in 1970 a director of Kinneir Calvert Tuhill. Her most notable achievements include designing the lettering and signing system for all the major airports in Britain which are run by the British Airports Authority; designing the Hockney book *Travels with Pen, Pencil and Ink,* which won the 1978 Design and Art Direction award for most outstanding book typography; and designing the Monotype Lasercomp typeface *Calvert,* which was adapted from the lettering she designed for the Tyne and Wear Metro. In 1983, Calvert was made a Fellow of the Royal College of Art where she has been teaching part-time for the past nineteen years. Calvert now runs her own design practice in London where she lives.

Tom Eckersley
Tom Eckersley studied at Salford School of Art where he met Eric Lombers. In 1934, they went to London and worked in collaboration until 1940. Their commissions included London Transport, Shell Mex and BP, General Post Office, and the BBC. Eckersley was visiting lecturer at Westminster School of Art from 1937 to 1939. During the war, he worked as a cartographer in the Royal Air Force, also designing many posters for the Royal Society for Prevention of Accidents and General Post Office, for which he was made Officer of the Order of the British Empire for services to British poster design. Since 1945, he has continued his design practice and involvement in teaching. From 1958 to 1976, Eckersley was head of the Design Department at the London College of Printing. His graphic work has been widely exhibited and is represented in many collections, including the Victoria and Albert Museum, the Imperial War Museum, the Museum of Modern Art, New York, and the Stedelijk Museum. In 1970, he was visiting lecturer at Yale University.

John Gorham
John Gorham worked as a designer at the British Printing Corporation and the *Sunday Times* before becoming art director with Cassons advertising agency. He subsequently set up his own freelance studio and for the past seventeen years has had his design practice in London, with a spell of teaching at the Royal College of Art. In 1984, the "Red Monarch" poster won the Creative Circle gold and silver awards, and a Design and Art Direction silver award. "The English Riviera" poster won a Creative Circle award.

F. H. K. Henrion
F. H. K. Henrion trained with Paul Colin in Paris. From 1936 to 1939, he worked in Paris and London. During World War II, he was consultant to the exhibitions division of the Ministry of Information and the U.S. Office of War Information in London. Henrion designed two pavilions for the 1951 Festival of Britain, and was art director for BOAC, and *Complete Imbiber, Contact,* and *Future* magazines. From 1955 to 1965, he was lecturer at the Royal College of Art. Henrion heads HDA International, consultants on corporate design. Henrion's experience in poster exhibitions, packaging, and magazine and book design led to specialization in design coordination, information design, and educational uses of audio-visual methods. From 1976 to 1979, Henrion was head of the Faculty of Visual Communications at the London College of Printing. Henrion received the silver star from Design and Art Direction in 1973 and in 1977 a design medal from the Society of Industrial Artists and Designers.

Mervyn Kurlansky
Educated at the Central School of Art, Mervyn Kurlansky started his own design practice in 1961. He was head of the graphic design department of Knoll International's Planning Unit before joining Crosby/Fletcher/Forbes in 1969. A founder-partner of Pentagram in 1972, he has since been responsible for major design programs for clients such as Prestel, a division of British Telecom, Reuters, Solaglas, and STC. His accolades include silver awards presented by the Designers' and Art Directors' Association of London. He is a fellow of the Society of Industrial Artists and Designers, and the Society of Typographic Designers.

Alan Fletcher
Alan Fletcher was educated at the Royal College of Art and Yale University. He began his career in New York, returning to London in 1962 to co-found Fletcher/Forbes/Gill. A founder-partner of Pentagram, his international reputation is demonstrated by the gold awards he has received from the Designers' and Art Directors' Association, London, and the New York One Show. President of the Designers' and Art Directors' Association in 1977, he shared with Colin Forbes the D&AD President's Award for outstanding contributions to design. In 1982, he was awarded the medal for outstanding achievement in industrial design by the Society of Industrial Artists and Designers. He was International President of the Alliance Graphique Internationale (1982–1985). Fletcher is represented in collections of major museums in Europe and the United States.

Milner Gray
Milner Gray studied painting and design at Goldsmith's College, London University. From 1934 to 1940, he taught at leading London art colleges and from 1937 to 1940 was principal of Sir John Cass College of Art and Design. From 1940 to 1944, he was head of the exhibitions branch and principal design advisor of the Ministry of Information. Gray designed the "Design at Home" (1945) and "Design at Work" (1948) exhibitions and was consultant to BBC schools broadcasts *Looking at Things* from 1949 to 1955. Designer of the British pavilion at the New York World's Fair in 1939, the "Britain Can Make It" exhibition (London, 1947), and the Festival of Britain (1951), Gray has designed corporate identity schemes for British Rail and was joint coordinating designer for the interior of the passenger liner *Oriana*. Gray was Master of the Faculty of Royal Designers for Industry from 1955 to 1957, and is founder-partner and senior consultant in the Design Research Unit, London.

David Hillman
Educated at the London College of Printing, David Hillman started his career as an assistant on the *Sunday Times* magazine. In 1968, he joined *Nova* magazine as art director and two years later became deputy editor. After the magazine's demise in 1975, he set up his own design practice in London and was commissioned to design the new French daily newspaper *Le Matin de Paris.* Since joining Pentagram in 1979, he has continued his editorial design work on publications including *Dinar* magazine, *Building, Sunday Express* magazine, *Nursing Times,* and *Information Resource Management.* He has also received numerous awards for his work in retail design and corporate identity. Hillman was appointed a Fellow of the Society of Industrial Artists and Designers in 1980.

John McConnell
Educated at Maidstone School of Art, John McConnell worked for advertising agencies before establishing his own graphic design practice in 1963. Responsible for the corporate identity for Biba, the influential sixties boutique store, he joined Pentagram in 1974. As main board director in charge of design and production at Faber & Faber publishers, he undertook the planning and commission of book jackets for over three hundred titles a year. He has won many international design awards, including the Designers' and Art Directors' Association President's Award in 1985, and serves regularly on juries all over the world. He is a member of the Post Office Stamp Advisory Committee, which advises on the issue of pictorial and commemorative British postage stamps. In June 1975, he was elected President of the Designers' and Art Directors' Association.

Harry Peccinotti
Apart from a two-year stint as a professional musician, Harry Peccinotti has worked in graphic design since 1950. Beginning at the age of fourteen as a trainee commercial artist, Peccinotti designed record sleeves for Esquire and Pye records, later moving into advertising as an art director/designer with various agencies. He was art director at *Nova* magazine (1963), where he first combined photography with graphic design. He has worked for *Twen, Vogue, Town, Elle,* and *Queen,* and did the photographs for the 1968 and 1969 Pirelli calendars. Peccinotti has received many awards from the art directors' clubs of London, Paris, and New York, and is presently working on a series of books and films on ethnic subjects.

Herbert Spencer
Herbert Spencer is a practicing designer and is consultant to several large companies and institutions in Britain, including the Tate Gallery, W. H. Smith, and British Rail. He is a director of Lund Humphries Publishers Ltd. In 1949, he founded the magazine *Typographica,* which he edited until 1967. He was the editor of *The Penrose Annual* from 1964 until 1973. In 1966, he was appointed Senior Research Fellow at the Royal College of Art in London to conduct a program of research into legibility in information publishing. He was Professor of Graphic Arts at the Royal College of Art from 1978 to 1984. Elected to the Faculty of Royal Designers for Industry in 1965, Spencer was International President of the Alliance Graphique Internationale from 1971 to 1974, and Master of the Faculty of Royal Designers for Industry from 1979 to 1981. He is a member of the British Post Office Stamp Advisory Committee. Spencer is the author of seven books including *Pioneers of Modern Typography* (Lund Humphries and MIT) and *The Visible Word* (Lund Humphries and Hastings House).

Frederick V. Carabott
Frederick V. Carabott studied in London at the Chelsea School of Art and at Saint Martin's School of Arts and Crafts from 1950 to 1953. Returning to his native Greece in 1957, he became art consultant to Aspiot-Elka Graphic Arts and *Pictures* magazine, both of Athens. Carabott has since acted in the same capacity for many other organizations including, until 1967, the Greek National Tourist Organization, which was awarded the Golden Tulip of the International Advertising Association in 1962 for work done largely under his direction. His poster designs, with a strong colorful style, have been very influential. In 1962, Carabott co-founded K + K Athens Publicity Center (now K + K/Univas). Carabott received the Livorno International Tourist Poster Exhibition award in 1962 and Rizzoli awards in 1964, 1965, 1966, and 1968. The King awarded him the Golden Cross of the Order of the Phoenix in recognition of outstanding contribution to graphic design in Greece. He now works freelance.

Henry Steiner
Henry Steiner has spent most of his working life in Hong Kong. He obtained an MFA from Yale University and spent a year with advertising agencies in New York before taking a Fulbright fellowship at the Sorbonne from 1958 to 1960. On his return to New York, he freelanced for periodicals including *Asia Magazine,* which he joined as design director in Hong Kong from 1961 to 1963. The following year, Steiner founded Graphic Communication Ltd., undertaking a comprehensive range of design work in Asia. He designed the graphics for the Hong Kong Hilton Hotel in 1963, and since 1967 has done the annual reports of the Hong Kong and Shanghai Banking Corporation. Steiner teaches at Hong Kong University and is president of the Hong Kong Chapter of the Society of Industrial Designers and Artists. He has won wide international acclaim including the Worldstar award in 1977. His work has been exhibited at Typomundus 20, and the Warsaw and Brno Biennales. His recent work includes the book *Yoshitoshi's Thirty-Six Ghosts.*

Michael Peters
Michael Peters graduated from the London College of Printing and received a master's degree from the Yale University School of Art and Architecture. Peters worked for CBS television in New York both on corporate and promotional projects, before returning to London in 1966 to join the advertising agency Collett, Dickenson, Pearce and Partners as creative director of the design department. In 1970, he founded Michael Peters and Partners of which he is chairman and creative director. Since its formation, the design firm has won many awards both nationally and internationally, including awards from the Designers' and Art Directors' Association and two silver awards from the New York Art Directors' Club.

Michael Katzourakis
Michael Katzourakis studied graphic design in Paris under Paul Colin and painting under André Lhote. In 1960, he became consultant to the Greek National Tourist Organization, and in 1962 was co-founder of K + K advertising agency, now K + K Univas. Katzourakis has concentrated on large-scale works that are integral to public spaces, including murals for banks, hotels, factories, and cruise ships. Parallel to this design work, he has been active as an artist, with ten one-man shows of painting and sculpture in Athens and Paris since 1969. He has received first and second prizes in Livorno international tourist poster competitions, and four Rizzoli awards.

Iran

Israel

Italy

Morteza Momayez
Morteza Momayez graduated from the Faculty of Fine Arts of the University of Tehran in 1964, and studied in Paris from 1965 to 1968. Illustrator and designer for Iranian newspapers and magazines already in the years from 1951 to 1958, he became designer and art director of Pars Studio and, in 1962, of Seven-Up Corporation. From 1962 to 1964, he was art director for the art magazine *The Book of the Week*. Art Director of *Rudaki* and *Life & Culture* magazines, from 1972 to 1978, Momayez lectured in the fine arts at Tehran and Farabi universities from 1969 to 1981. From 1974 to 1978, he was art manager and designer for the Tehran International Film Festival and in 1971, 1972, and 1973 directed three short animation films. Momayez has had eight one-man exhibitions in Tehran and has participated in recent years at the Poster Biennale in Warsaw, the Graphic Biennale in Brno, and at group shows in Bologna, Paris, and Chicago.

Jean David
Jean David was born in Rumania, studied in Paris, fled Europe on a sailing boat in 1942, and settled in Israel in 1948, where he became the government adviser on industrial design. He painted murals for public buildings, including the University Campus in Jerusalem, the University and Rothschild Hospital in Haifa, Weizman Institute of Science in Rehovot, and the Israeli pavilions at the Brussels and Montreal World Fairs. His work on the interiors of the seven Israeli passenger ships includes two 50-meter stained-glass windows for the *Shalom*. Posters for the Israeli Ministry of Tourism won gold and silver medals at the 1954 Milan Triennale. Foremost a painter, Jean David has had one-man exhibitions in London, Paris, New York, Mexico City, Johannesburg, and Bucharest.

Yarom Vardimon
Yarom Vardimon studied graphic design in England at Regent Polytechnic and the London College of Printing, from which he graduated in 1964. Vardimon specializes in design of corporate identity programs, packaging, and typography, and has gained more than thirty awards in national competitions. Elected president of Israel Graphic Designers' Association in 1969, he was vice-president of the International Council of Graphic Design Associations from 1974 to 1979. Also active in the field of design education, he contributes to *Israel Design* magazine. He is Professor of Graphic Communication and, since 1977, Chairman of the Graphic Design Department at Bezalel Academy, Jerusalem, which he joined in 1968. Vardimon is visiting lecturer at Ravensbourne College and Saint Martin's School of Art and Design in England, and the Graphic School and the School for Applied Arts in Denmark. His work has appeared in *Idea, Print, Communication Arts, Novum, Graphic Design,* and *Graphis.*

Walter Ballmer
Walter Ballmer studied in Lucerne and at the Kunstgewerbeschule in Basel. In 1947, he went to Milan to work in the Boggeri design studio. In 1948, Ballmer set up his own design practice, working for clients including Pirelli, La Roche, Geigy, Montecatini, and Olivetti. In 1956, he joined Olivetti, entering their department of public relations, industrial design, and advertising, where over the years he has designed graphics, packaging, murals, displays, and exhibitions. His work has been exhibited internationally, and he has received many awards including the gold medal conferred on him at the Ljubljana Bio 5 (1973) for his Olivetti Image exhibition. His work is represented in the permanent collection of the National Museum, Warsaw.

Dan Reisinger
Dan Reisinger began his career in 1958, when his poster "International Science Pavilion—Expo 58" won first prize at Brussels Expo. He continued as a poster artist in London for General Post Office and other national institutions, opening his own design studio in Tel Aviv in 1966. Since then his work has covered all aspects of graphic design and includes supergraphics and environmental projects. Reisinger has designed symbols and corporate identity programs for major companies and institutions in Israel, notably El-Al Israel Airlines and Habima, Israel's National Theater. His calendars and posters have won many international awards. Formerly professor in the department of design at Haifa University, he teaches at the Bezalel Academy of Art, Jerusalem, his alma mater. Reisinger has gained recognition for the *Scrolls of Fire*, a series of fifty-three paintings permanently on exhibition at the Diaspora Museum, Tel Aviv. One-man shows of his paintings have also been held in San Diego, London, Brussels, and at the Jewish Museum in New York.

Franco Bassi
Franco Bassi studied at the Accademia di Belle Arti di Brera, then taught for some years at Istituto d'Arte, Cantù. He joined Olivetti in 1949 and is now art director in one of Olivetti's design and advertising studios. He has also been art director at Weisscredit, Lugano, and Italconsult, Rome. Clients include Edizioni di Comunità, Electa Editrice, and Eurallumina. Bassi had one-man exhibitions in Milan in 1946, 1948, and 1949, and took part in the exhibition of abstract and concrete art in Milan in 1947, and the first international biennale devoted to form in human environment in Rimini in 1969. In the same year, he was awarded *Il Tempo*'s Trofeo d'oro, and the Mondadori and *Il Giorno* prizes at the second exhibition of the Art Director's Club, Milan. Bassi received the gold medal in 1973 at the Ljubljana industrial design biennale. His work has appeared in many national and international graphics periodicals.

Egidio Bonfante

Egidio Bonfante studied at the Brera Academy and the architecture school of the Milan Polytechnic. He was editor of a number of periodicals dealing with arts and letters, including *Posizione* (Novara, 1942–1943), *Numero* and *Il Ventaglio* (Novara, 1946), and was on the editorial staff of *A, Arredamento* (Milan, 1946), *Communità* (Ivrca-Milan, 1946–1970), and *Urbanistica* (Turin, 1946–1967). He is the author of *Considerazioni sulla pittura dei giovani* [Thoughts on the Painting of the Young] (Milan, 1946) and, under the pseudonym Jacopo Robusti, *L'Amour peintre* (Milan, 1969). In collaboration with Juti Ravenna, he published *Cinquanta disegni di Picasso* [Fifty Drawings by Picasso] (Novarra, 1943) and *Arte cubista* [Cubist Art] (Venice, 1945). He was a member of the Realism Beyond Guernica Movement in Milan, 1946. Since 1940, he has shown in many Italian and international exhibitions, including the Venice Biennale and has had numerous one-man shows of graphic work, painting, and collages. Since 1948, he has been a designer with Olivetti Advertising office.

Pierluigi Cerri

Pierluigi Cerri has been a contributor to the magazine *Lotus International* and is editor of *Casabella* and *Rassegna*, as well as art director at Electa Editrice. Graduate in architecture, he has edited many publications, including the Italian edition of Le Corbusier's *Vers une architecture, Autentico ma contraffatto* (1976), *Pubblicità d'autore* (1983), and the graphics series *Pagina*. He has designed many exhibitions in Europe including Peter Behrens and AEG in Berlin; Carrozzeria Italiana in Turin, Rome, and Los Angeles; Identité Italienne at the Pompidou Center in Paris; Alexander Calder in Turin in 1983; Italian Furniture Design in Stuttgart in 1983 and in Tokyo in 1984; and Venti progetti per il futuro del lingotto in Turin in 1984. He is responsible for the image of Palazzo Grassi in Venice. A partner of Gregotti Associates, he is in charge of design and communications.

Silvio Coppola

Silvio Coppola graduated in architecture from Politecnico di Milan and has since worked primarily in this field, designing department stores and offices in Baghdad (1956–1958), and residential accommodations for several Italian towns. Architect since 1965 with European Development Fund, Coppola has been responsible for many projects including four complete student residential complexes in Zaire. His architectural activity has been paralleled by his work in interior design. His designs are in the collections of Bernini, Tigamma, Montina, Mobel Italiana, Cilsa, Alessi, Tessitura di Mompiano, Tronconi, Clerion, I.C.M., Artemide, and Cassina. Coppola has worked as a freelance designer and consultant for communication and design for major Italian and European firms. Since 1967, he has been a member of the Exhibition Design research group. Since 1975, he has taught design at the Accademia di Belle Arti di Carrara, and since 1976 at the Essen-Gesamthochschule. His work is represented in the collections of the Museum of Modern Art, New York, and the Georges Pompidou Center, Paris.

Italo Lupi

Italo Lupi did his studies in architecture at Milan Polytechnic. Based in Milan, he is currently involved in graphic design and visual communication and in exhibition architecture design. He has taught graphic design at ISIA, Urbino, and was assistant to Pier Giacomo Castiglioni in drawing at Milan Polytechnic. Lupi has been art director for the magazines *Abitare, Costruire, Zodiac, Shop, Il Verde di Abitare,* and *Il Giornale della Lombardia.* Designer of the image of the Triennale di Milano, he is consultant for various manufacturing concerns and political and civil bodies. He is editor of the new guide published by the Lombardy government to its nineteen regional parks, including the Ticino Valley. Lupi received first prize for editorial design from the Art Directors' Club of Milan in 1978.

Mimmo Castellano

Mimmo Castellano is self-taught as an artist. After having lived for fifteen years in South Italy, he started his professional career in 1950. He worked as a scenographer with the producer Anton Guilio Bragaglia and later with Compagnia Stabile di Prosa della Città di Bari. In the book sector, he cooperated with the publisher Laterza, Carlo Ludovico Ragghianti, Umberto Ecco, and Leonardo Sinisgalli. He designed, together with Achille Pier Giacomo and Livio Castiglioni, the Italian Radio and Television pavilions in 1956 in Bari, and in 1967 in Milan. In 1970, he held the Graphic Design chair at the Academy of Fine Arts in Bari and from 1980 to 1981 at ISIA in Urbino. Since 1956, he has won numerous awards, including two prizes for culture and photography for the books *London* and *Noi Vivi* in 1965 and 1966. Since 1967, Castellano has lived and worked in Milan.

Giulio Cittato

Giulio Cittato graduated from Venice University in 1963, then spent two years as designer with La Rinascente in Milan. In 1965, he moved to the United States where he worked as a designer for Unimark International, the Center for Advanced Research in Design, and Container Corporation of America. Since his return to Venice in 1971, he has been involved in a wide range of design projects, including corporate image programs and signage, both of which he has taught at the Graphic Design University in Urbino from 1978 to 1980. From 1971 to 1974, he taught visual design at the Corso Superiore di Disegno Industriale and the International University of Art in Venice. Cittato had a one-man exhibition at the Smithsonian Institute in 1969, and has participated in poster exhibitions in Milan, Montreal, and Venice. His work is represented in the collection of the Museum of Modern Art, New York, and various museums in Italy and abroad.

Franco Grignani

Franco Grignani studied architecture, but his work has always been devoted to experimentation in optical and visual phenomena applied to painting, graphic design, and photographs. Grignani spent many years as art director of *Bellezza d'Italia*. Since 1956, he has been art director of *Pubblicità in Italia*. He has had more than forty-nine one-man exhibitions since 1958 in Italy, Great Britain, Switzerland, Germany, the United States, and Venezuela. His works have been shown in numerous international exhibitions, including all Warsaw Poster Biennales, where he won an award in 1966, and the Venice Biennale in 1972. Grignani was winner of the Palma d'Oro della Pubblicità in 1959 and the gold medal at the Milan Triennale. His works have been acquired by museums in Rome, Milan, Livorno, Parma, Florence, Verona, Hamburg, and Caracas.

Emanuele Luzzati

Emanuele Luzzati studied in Lausanne before beginning a career as theater designer in 1946. He has since designed sets for more than two hundred fifty plays, operas, and ballets, and published some fifty theater posters. Luzzati has also designed material for theater and opera companies in the United States and Europe. Outstanding achievements include design of sets and costumes for Mozart's *Magic Flute* at the 1963 Glyndebourne Festival. Since 1960, he has been involved primarily in illustration and cartoon films, writing and illustrating books for children, and producing cartoons in collaboration with Giulio Gianini. Two of his films are in the collection of the Museum of Modern Art, New York, and two others were nominated for the American film Oscar.

Armando Milani

Armando Milani studied at Scuola Umanitaria in Milan under Albe Steiner and, after collaborating with some of the most important design studios, became freelance in the 1970s. In 1976, he left Milan for New York where he spent two years with Massimo Vignelli, subsequently setting up his own studio, leaving his brother Maurizio in charge of the studio in Milan. He specializes in corporate identity programs, book design, and work for cultural institutions, designing logos, posters, ads, and packaging. Milani won an award in 1965 with his design of the logo for Radiotelefortuna. In 1983, he taught Graphic Design at the Cooper Union School in New York. His work has been included in major exhibitions in Milan, Paris, New York, Montreal, and Los Angeles, and has been widely published.

Bob Noorda

Bob Noorda studied at Amsterdam Institute of Design. He has specialized in signage systems, corporate image programs, and related branches of advertising. Noorda designed signage for subways in Milan, New York, and São Paulo. Clients have included Agip, Mitsubishi, Spear & Jackson, Stella-Artois, Chiari & Forti, Feltrinelli, Upim, Mondadori, Total, Shiseido, Olivetti, and Touring Club Italiano. In 1961, Noorda became art director of Pirelli and in 1965 co-founder and senior vice-president for design and marketing of Unimark International Corporation. He received a Gold Compass for the Milan subway system signage, gold medals in Rimini in 1968, Ljubljana in 1973, and at the 13th Milan Triennale. Noorda was a member of the commission of the International Council of Societies of Industrial Design for research in visual communication from 1968 to 1970 and has since 1975 been a member of the scientific committee of Istituto Superiore per il Disegno Grafico in Urbino.

Heinz Waibl

Heinz Waibl studied at the Liceo Artistico and the Politecnico in Milan where he now lives and works. In 1974, he founded SIGNO, a design firm specializing in graphic design and visual communication. From 1950 to 1954, he was assistant to Max Huber, with whom he began the teaching program for graphic designers at Umanitaria, Milan. For ten years, Waibl worked freelance, in 1967 going to the United States to be executive designer at Unimark Corporation. Waibl worked in New York, Chicago, and South Africa until 1971, when he returned to Milan where he was subsequently appointed chairman of visual design at the Scuola Politecnica di Design. His major clients include American Airlines, Brion Vega, Cizano, Flos, Italia Nostra, Max Meyer, Motta, JC Penny, Nava Milano, Porsche Design, RAI, Rank Xerox, Rinascente, Transunion Corporation, and Venini. Waibl has created a line of diaries called "Impatto" for Nava Milano which has been selected for New York's Museum of Modern Art catalogue.

Shigeo Fukuda

Shigeo Fukuda graduated in 1956 from Tokyo National University of Art and Music. His design work, which is characterized by illusion and humor, includes illustration, symbol-trademark sculpture, environmental design, and ceramics. Since 1966, he has participated in major international graphic arts and poster exhibitions. He has had one-man exhibitions in New York, Italy, France, and Japan. Fukuda's work is represented in the Museum of Modern Art, New York, and collections in Colorado, Paris, and Moscow. He has taught at Tokyo University of Arts and Yale University.

Bruno Monguzzi

Bruno Monguzzi studied at the Ecole des Arts Décoratifs in Geneva, and then in London. In 1961, he joined Studio Boggeri in Milan, designing for Pirelli, Roche, Loro and Parisini. From 1963 to 1965, he taught typographic design at the Cini Foundation in Venice. In 1965, Monguzzi went to Montreal to design nine pavilions for Expo '67. Since 1968, he has designed books, catalogues, hospital signage, and exhibits, often in collaboration with Roberto Sambonet. In association with the Paris office Visuel Design Jean Widmer, Monguzzi won the international competition for the Musée d'Orsay signage system in 1983. Professor of typographic design and the psychology of perception at the Lugano School for the Applied Arts since 1971, in 1981 he was IBM Fellow at the Aspen Design Conference and, the following year, visiting professor at Cooper Union in New York. Awarded the Premio Bodoni in 1971, Monguzzi is author of *Lo Studio Boggeri 1933–1981* and *Piet Zwart typographer.*

Roberto Sambonet

Roberto Sambonet graduated in architecture from the Università degli Studi, Milan. He began work as a painter and portraitist in Stockholm with an exhibition of his work in 1947, followed by exhibitions in Venice, Milan, Turin, São Paulo, Rio de Janeiro, and Helsinki. In the 1950s, Sambonet worked under P. M. Bardi in Brazil, and Alvaro Aalto in Finland. Formerly art director for the architecture revue *Zodiac,* he has drawn plans for Pirelli, Einaudi, Feltrinelli, La Rinascente, Triennale, Pinacotece di Brera, Regione Lombardia (Compasso d'Oro, 1979), and Touring Club Italiano. As a designer, he has worked for Baccarat, Sambonet, Bing & Grondhal, Richard Ginori, and Seguso Murano. He has been awarded the Compasso d'Oro (1956 and 1970), the Domus Inxo Award, and the Gran Premio at the 12th Triennale. Sambonet taught design at the Academy of Carrara. His work is represented in the Museum of Modern Art, New York. He lives and works in Milan.

Takenobu Igarashi

Takenobu Igarashi graduated from Tama University of Fine Arts in Tokyo in 1968, and obtained a master's degree in design from the University of California in Los Angeles in 1969. He established Igarashi Studio in Tokyo in 1970. A graphic designer and sculptor, Igarashi conducts an international design practice ranging from print media to environmental design. His work includes corporate identity programs, signage, and environmental planning. Igarashi is well known for his axonometric posters using three-dimensional alphabets. Igarashi served as guest professor at the University of California, where he taught graphic design from 1975 to 1976. He also taught design in the Engineering Department of Chiba University in Japan from 1979 to 1983. His works have been exhibited at various universities and conferences, including the Smithsonian Institution in Washington, D.C., the University of Hawaii, and the Art Center College of Design. Igarashi's works are included in the collection of the Museum of Modern Art, New York.

Japan   Mexico   Netherlands

Yusaku Kamekura
Yusaku Kamekura studied at the Institute
of New Architecture and Industrial Arts,
focusing his attention on the basic theory
of composition. He joined International
Industrial Arts Information Company in
1983 and was appointed art director of the
English-language magazine *Nippon,*
which was instrumental in introducing
Japanese culture overseas. Founder-
member in 1960 and currently director of
Japan Design Center, Kamekura serves
as chairman of the Japan Graphic
Designer Association. Early important exhibitions include Graphic 55 and a one-
man show at Normandy House, Chicago,
sponsored by the Chicago Typographic
Art Society. Since 1962, Kamekura has
worked freelance. For his design of the
Tokyo Olympic Games symbol in 1961,
he received the grand prize of the Ministry
of Education. He designed a series of
Olympic posters for Expo '70, and in 1978
designed the symbol and poster for
Interski '79. Between 1957 and 1972,
Kamekura received a special, four gold,
five silver, and several copper medals and
member prizes from the Tokyo Art
Directors' Club.

Kazumasa Nagai
Kazumasa Nagai left the sculpture
department of Tokyo University of Fine
Arts and Music in 1951. In 1960, he entered Nippon Design Center, where he is
now president. In 1966 and 1972, Nagai
won the competition for the symbols of the
Sapporo Winter Olympics and the
Okinawa International Ocean Exposition.
He was awarded the Membership Award
and a silver and four bronze medals
from the Art Directors' Club of Tokyo from
1960 to 1983. Recent prizes include the
Mainichi Design Award, the silver medal
of the Sign-Display Association and of the
Japanese Lettering Annual, and numerous medals and prizes at the International
Poster Biennale in Warsaw, and the Inter-
national Graphic Art Biennale in Brno.
Nagai's work is represented in collections
of the Tokyo and Kyoto national museums
of modern art, the Museum of Modern Art,
New York, the Metropolitan Museum of
Art, New York, and the Australia National
Gallery, Canberra.

Félix Beltrán
Félix Beltrán apprenticed with McCann-
Erikson in Havana before traveling to the
United States in 1956. After working for
various studios and publications, he
studied graphic design, painting, and
engraving at schools in New York. Beltrán
returned to Cuba in 1962 and set up a
consultancy designing posters, publications, and exhibitions for various organizations. He was design director for the
Cuban Pavilion at Expo '67 in Montreal,
and painter of twenty-six murals for Expo
'70 in Osaka. In 1964, he introduced
Cuba's first basic design course at the
National School of Industrial Design in
Havana. Since 1962, there have been
fifty-two one-man exhibitions of his work
held around the world. He has participated in over four hundred collective exhibitions, and is represented in the collections
of fifty-three museums worldwide. In
1984, he assumed Mexican citizenship,
and is currently titular professor of the
Metropolitan Autonomous University, and
the National School of Design, in Mexico.

Ben Bos
Ben Bos started his career as a journalist
and copywriter. He worked for nine years
for the Dutch firm Ahrend, where he became art director after studying graphic
design with Wim Crouwel and other leading designers at the Rietveld Academy
in Amsterdam. When Crouwel, Benno
Wissing, and Frisno Kramer founded
Total Design in 1963, Bos was invited to
join them. In 1967, he was appointed to
the Total Design board. Bos has taught at
Ravensbourne College in England, and
Rietveld Academy. A lecturer at universities in Europe, Japan, and the United
States, he has received text and design
awards in the Netherlands, and at Brno,
Prague, Sofia, Ljubljana, and Vienna. Still
strongly influenced by his writing career,
he often works for newspapers and magazines. His design work includes trademarks, corporate identity programs, and
stamps. He is also a photographer.

Mitsuo Katsui
Mitsuo Katsui graduated from Tokyo University in 1955. He joined the Ajinomoto
Company in 1956 and became freelance
in 1961. Katsui specializes in the design of
maps, diagrams, and calendars, with
emphasis on the development of abstract
forms. In 1965, he produced the animated
film *GMP 65* using mechanically produced geome patterns. Katsui participated in Expo '70 as art director of Orgorama
Government Pavilion No. 2 and of
Kodansha's World's Biggest Picture Book
exhibition. Katsui helped organize the
Persona Coterie exhibition in 1965, where
the group won the Mainichi Industrial
Design prize, and an environmental
exhibition in 1966. He has participated in
biennales in Warsaw and Brno and other
group shows in Japan, the Netherlands,
and in 1980 in London. He won a second
Mainichi prize in 1975, and awards from
the Lettering Institute and the Typography
Institute in 1969 and 1971. Katsui is lecturer of design at Tsukuba University in
Japan.

Ikko Tanaka
Ikko Tanaka graduated from Kyoto
Municipal College of Arts and Crafts in
1950 and joined Kenegafuchi Spinning
Mills as textile designer. From 1952 to
1957, he worked as graphic designer with
Sankei Press, then moved to Tokyo and
taught until 1965 at Kuwazawa Institute of
Design. Tanaka was art director at Nippon
Design Center until 1963 before opening
his own design studio. In 1970, he worked
on the Japanese History Pavilion at Expo
'70 in Osaka. His exhibition at Matsuya,
Tokyo, in 1973 recorded twenty years of
poster design for Kanze Noh drama.
Tanaka designed the "Japan Style" exhibition at the Victoria and Albert Museum
(1980), and the "Japan Design–Tradi-
tional and Contemporary" exhibition in
Moscow (1984). He has been the recipient of numerous awards from the Tokyo
Art Directors' Club. Since 1973, Tanaka
has been art director of the Seibu Retail
Group.

Pieter Brattinga
Pieter Brattinga began his career as director of design at Steendrukkerij De Jong
in Hilversum. From 1955 to 1974, he was
editor of *Quadrat Prints* in Hilversum. In
1961, he was named chairman of the department of visual communication at Pratt
Institute in New York. From 1966 to 1970,
he was secretary general of Icograda and
from 1968 to 1971 president of the
Netherlands Art Directors' Club. Between
1966 and 1970, he coordinated the editing of *Novivorm*, the design manual for the
chemical concern DSM Netherlands. In
the years 1969, 1971, 1973, 1980, and
1981, he designed stamps for the Netherlands Postal Service. He created posters
and catalogues for the exhibitions at the
Kröller-Müller Museum, and from 1973 to
1980 he supervised and coordinated the
design of the signage of the Amsterdam
Metro. In 1974, Brattinga began to show a
series of experimental prints in his gallery
in Amsterdam. He had one-man exhibitions in Minneapolis in 1963, in Lodz in
1974, in Berlin in 1976, and in Otterlo in
1980.

Dick Bruna
Dick Bruna, self-taught artist, has designed more than two thousand book jackets and posters since 1945. In 1971 and 1975, he created a series of posters for the Dutch Dairy Council, for which he won prizes from the Art Director's Club and Genootschap van Reclame, and from the Toronto poster exhibition. In 1969, Bruna designed children's stamps for the Dutch postal authorities and in 1974, a campaign for the Netherlands Red Cross. He has developed a series of packaging for Nestlé in cooperation with Pieter Brattinga. His forty-two picture books for young children have appeared in nineteen languages, and five of them have been chosen Best Children's Book of the year. In 1977, an exhibition was held in the Gemmentemuseum in Arnheim based on the character of Miffy.

Otto H. Treumann
Otto H. Treumann was trained at the Amsterdam Grafische School and Nieuwe Kunstschool from 1935 to 1940. Since 1945, he has had his own studio, designing for El Al airlines, Nederlandse Gasunie, Wolters-Noordhoff Publishers, Utrecht Industries Fair, Bijenkorf department store, Delft Technical University, Association of Netherlands architects, Philips, National Savings Bank, Sonsbeek Open Air Exhibitions, and the Institute for Psychotechnique. He has also designed twenty postage stamps for the Netherlands Post Office. From 1946 to 1959, he did the layout for the *Rayon Revue,* which gained him the Werkman prize in 1947 and the Duwaer prize in 1957. Board member of the Rietveld Academy, Amsterdam, and Bezalel Academy, Jerusalem, Treumann has long been chairman of GKF Society of graphic designers in the Netherlands. Among many other awards, Treumann has received the D. A. Thieme prize in 1960 and the David Röell prize in 1970.

Bruno Oldani
Bruno Oldani studied graphic design at P. O. Althaus Advertising Agency, Zurich, and the City of Zurich School of Art and Design. Oldani studied industrial design at the State School of Art and Craft in Oslo. From 1958 to 1964, Oldani worked as a graphic designer at design studios in Oslo. In 1965, he set up his own studio in Oslo with a team of associates, working in the fields of graphic and typographic design, corporate identity programs, publication design, exhibition planning and design, information and signaling systems, book and record-cover design, television graphics, and advertising campaigns. Oldani's international clients include IBM, SAS (Catering Division), Philips, Letraset, and the City of Kiel, West Germany. He is four-time first-prize winner of the international Premio Rizzoli.

Jan Mlodozeniec
Jan Mlodozeniec studied graphics at Warsaw Academy of Fine Arts. Since 1952, he has done book jackets and illustrations for the publishers Czytelnik, PIW, Iskry, and Ksiazka i Wiedza. Mlodozeniec specializes in cultural publicity, designing posters for the publisher WAG, the Central Office for Film Distribution, and opera, theater, and ballet companies. His satirical drawings appear in *Miesiecznik Literacki,* and he has also contributed to *Nowa Kultura, Ekran,* and *Film.* He has had one-man exhibitions in Warsaw, Prague, Vienna, Berlin, Stockholm, Lahti, and Aosta since 1962. Since 1966, his work has appeared at the international poster exhibitions in Warsaw, Brno, Lahti, Colorado, and Toyama. Recipient of numerous awards and prizes, Mlodozeniec has his work represented in collections in the Poster Museum, Wilanów, the National Museum, Poznán, the Stedelijk Museum, the Musée de L'Affiche, Paris, and the Museum of Contemporary Art, Kamakura, Japan.

Wim Crouwel
Wim Crouwel was trained at the Academy of Arts and Crafts, Groningen, and the Institute for Arts and Crafts, Amsterdam. He started his design practice in 1952 and taught at the Royal Academy of Arts and Crafts, 's Hertogenbosch, until 1957. From then until 1960, he collaborated with designer Kho Liang Ie. Crouwel taught at the Institute for Arts and Crafts, Amsterdam, from 1957 to 1963, and was among the designers of the Dutch pavilion at the 1970 Osaka World's Fair. Secretary general of Icograda from 1963 to 1966, Crouwel founded Total Design in 1963 with four other designers. He has been a graphic designer for the Stedelijk Museum since 1964, has taught at Delft University of Technology (1965–1978), and was professor there during the years 1972–1978 and 1980–1985. He is presently director of the Museum Boymans-van Beuningen in Rotterdam. The recipient of many prizes for poster and book design, Crouwel had an exhibition of his work at the Stedelijk Museum in 1979.

Jan van Toorn
A freelance designer in Amsterdam since 1957, Jan van Toorn has been teaching graphic design and visual communication at Gerrit Rietveld Academy, Amsterdam, since 1967. He has taught at other schools, including Amsterdam University and Technical University, Eindhoven. A designer for Van Abbemuseum, Eindhoven, from 1967 to 1973, van Toorn's work there included the exhibition "The Street," also shown in Germany, Austria, and Sweden in 1972. Van Toorn designed the Dutch contribution "Beyond Shelter" to the Venice Biennale in 1976. He is co-editor and designer of the book *Museum in Motion?* (The Hague, 1979). His recent works include several series of stamps for the Dutch Postal Services, an exhibition center on the delta plan for the State Public Works Department, and a design for the International Department of the Netherlands Office for Fine Arts.

Franciszek Starowieyski
Franciszek Starowieyski studied painting from 1949 to 1955 in Warsaw and Cracow, at the same time that he was drawing cartoons, posters, and illustrated books. In the last twenty-five years, he has published some two hundred posters, whose singularity of theme stems from a preoccupation with monstrosity and from a style owing its main features to Renaissance drawing. He has also designed stage decors and is devoted to baroque calligraphy. In 1971, Starowieyski made the award-winning film *Bykowi chwala* (Glory to the Bull). Since 1974, he has frequently been invited by the Kosciusko Foundation to work in New York. In 1980, he was visiting professor at the Berliner Hochschule der Künste. Starowieyski has received more than ten Best Poster awards at Warsaw and Poznán, prizes at the Biennale of São Paulo in 1973 and at the Filmposter Exhibition in Cannes in 1974, and first prize at the Annual Key Award in Los Angeles in 1978.

Poland

Spain

Waldemar Swierzy
Waldemar Swierzy studied at the Katowice College of Arts and the Cracow Academy of Art. In 1952, he moved to Warsaw where he has worked for the WAG publishing house and the CWP film distributors. While concentrating on producing posters, he has illustrated many books and also designed a number of exhibitions for the Polish Chamber of Commerce in Warsaw and in other cities. Since 1965, Swierzy has been a lecturer at the School of Art in Poznán. He has had one-man shows in Europe as well as in Havana, Caracas, and Mexico. Winner of a silver medal in 1972 and a gold medal in 1976 at the Warsaw Poster Biennale, Swierzy also received the Hollywood Reporter first prize in 1975, and the gold medal at the Lahti Poster Biennale in 1977. Examples of his work are in the Stedelijk Museum, and other museums in New York, Moscow, and Malmö.

Maciej Urbaniec
Maciej Urbaniec studied in Wroclaw at the Academy of Plastic Arts from 1952 to 1954, and from 1954 to 1958 at the Academy of Fine Arts in Warsaw. He specializes in poster design and since 1960 has taken part in all Polish poster exhibitions. Since 1958 design consultant to WAG art publishers in Warsaw, Urbaniec has lectured at Wroclaw Academy of Plastic Arts since 1970 and at Warsaw Academy of Fine Arts since 1975. Urbaniec has had one-man exhibitions in Warsaw (1968, 1975), Szczecin (1969), Poznán and Radom (1975), and Kielce (1976). Urbaniec won the Tadeusz Trepkowski prize in 1958, first prize in the national competition for posters to commemorate the fifteenth anniversary of the Polish People's Republic, first prize in competition for the Poster for Peace in 1970, and thirteen prizes for Best Poster at Warsaw from 1964 to 1980. Urbaniec's work is represented in the collections of the Georges Pompidou Center and the Stedelijk Museum.

Enric Huguet
Enric Huguet graduated from schools of fine and applied arts in Barcelona. Since 1956, he has worked as a freelance graphic designer and is currently consultant to Sociedad de Aguas de Barcelona, Roca Radiadores, Autopistas Concesionaria Española, Laboratorios Bama, J. Uriach y Cia., Bibliograf, Casa Santiveri, and Salón Náutico Internacional de Barcelona. Founder-member of Agrupación Diseño Gráfico del FAD in 1961, since 1963 Huguet has taught graphics at Escuela Massaña, Barcelona. He was awarded Deltas de Plata from Agrupación Diseño Industrial del FAD in 1962 and 1963, and the Trofeo Laus from the ADG in 1973. Works of his are to be found in the Museo de Arte Moderno in Barcelona, the Museum of Pescia, Italy, and the Berlin Museum.

José Pla-Narbona
José Pla-Narbona studied at art school in Barcelona, then lived in Paris from 1956 to 1958. On his return, he opened his own studio and in 1961 was appointed to teach advertising art at Escuela Massaña. His work covers a wide range of graphic and applied art. He has had one-man exhibitions in Barcelona, Zurich, New York, Chicago, and the Hague. Winner of the Sant Jordi prize for drawing in 1960 and for painting in 1961, Pla-Narbona was awarded first prize for poster design at the 2nd International Applied Arts Biennale in Punta del Este, Uruguay in 1967, and first prize at the International Drawing Competition, Ynglada-Guillot, in 1976. His work is represented in the collection of the Baltimore Museum of Art and the museums of modern art in New York, San Francisco, and Los Angeles. Collectors Press of San Francisco and Ferdinand Roten of Maryland have entrusted him with a series of lithographs and etchings.

Henryk Tomaszewski
Henryk Tomaszewski studied at the Academy of Fine Arts, Warsaw, from 1934 to 1939. After World War II, he resumed work as a graphic artist for Polish publishers and cultural institutions as a stage designer. He has taught in the department of poster design at Warsaw Academy since 1952. His works, which have been exhibited in all parts of the world, have earned him many awards, including gold and silver medals at the 1st and 4th Warsaw Biennales, first prize at the 1963 São Paulo Biennale, a gold medal at the Leipzig Book Fair in 1965, and first prize at the Colorado International Invitational Poster Exhibition in 1981. His children's books have received official recognition from the Polish government. Tomaszewski was awarded a prize for his satirical drawings by *Przeglad Kulturalny* magazine in 1961. His work is represented in the collections of the Museum of Modern Art, New York, and the Museum of Contemporary Art, Kamakura, Japan.

Fernando Medina
After working as art director in various advertising agencies, Fernando Medina set up his own practice in Madrid in 1970, devoting his energies to visual communication and, more particularly, corporate identity programs. In 1985, he moved to Montreal, which afforded a wider scope to his activities, and opened his own office, Medina Design. Visiting professor at the University of Quebec in Montreal, his work has been exhibited at the Colorado International Poster Exhibition (1981), the 10th International Poster Biennale in Poland, the Typo-Graphisme Exhibition (1985) at the Pompidou Center, and the Lahti Poster Biennale (1985). Medina has received awards from the Art Directors' Club of Los Angeles, the Type Directors' Club of New York, and Communications Art Annual.

Tomás Vellvé
Tomás Vellvé started work in 1942 as a draftsman at Rieusset S.A., Barcelona, where he gained experience in printing and reproduction techniques while studying drawing, typography, photography, and printmaking. In 1948, he moved to Madrid to continue his studies in the fine and graphic arts. He was commissioned in 1970 by Neufville typographers to design a new typeface, *Premier jambage sec ibérique,* subsequently known as *Vellvé.* Since 1963, he has exhibited many times in Barcelona and has participated, since 1959, in international exhibitions in Canada, the United States, Eastern and Western Europe, Israel, and Brazil. Vellvé represented Spain at the international congress in Montreal in 1965. He has received numerous awards, including first poster awards in 1956, 1958, and 1967; and many prizes for graphics. Examples of his work are in public collections in Berlin, Honolulu, Warsaw, Barcelona, Belgrade, Brno, Dublin, and New York.

Olle Eksell

Olle Eksell worked as a window decorator while studying under Hugo Steiner-Prague in Stockholm from 1939 to 1941. He worked for the advertising agency Ervaco until 1945 and spent a year at the Los Angeles Art Center School. Eksell organized the first American graphic design exhibition at the National Museum, Stockholm, in 1947. In 1969, he founded Olle Eksell Design AB. Also active in book design and cartoon illustration, since 1952 he has worked as a writer and illustrator for the newspaper *Aftonbladet*. Guest speaker at the International Design Conference, Aspen, in 1960, and jury member for Typomundus 20 in Toronto in 1964, Eksell has received numerous first prizes in design contests. His book *Design-Ekonomi* won a silver medal in Leipzig in 1965, and in 1972 he was awarded a grant from the Swedish Author's Foundation to write a book analyzing visual location of streets, public buildings, work places, subway stations, and highways. In 1974, Eksell was awarded the largest Swedish artist state grant.

Donald Brun

Donald Brun received his training in a graphic art studio in Basel and at the Akademie für freie und angewandte Kunst in Berlin, where he studied under O. H. W. Hadank and Professor Böhm. He established his own studio in Basel in 1933 and has since specialized in advertising art, including work for the chemical industry in Basel and other commercial enterprises. He created two pavilions for the Swiss National Exhibition in Zurich in 1939, and designed the cultural section and Swiss chemistry exhibition stands at the Brussels World Fair in 1958. Each year he produces exhibition material for the Swiss Industries Fair in Basel, and a number of his designs are used regularly in the fashion sections of this exhibition. He works as a poster artist with many international firms in the United States, Germany, England, Austria, Italy, and the Benelux countries. From 1947 to 1974, he taught graphic art at the Kunstgewerbeschule in Basel. He is holder of several awards for Best Swiss Poster.

Karl Domenig Geissbühler

Karl Domenig Geissbühler studied under Ernst Keller at the Kunstgewerbeschule in Zurich. Geissbühler also attended the Kunstakademie in Berlin. He spent five years as art director with the Rudolf Farner Advertising Agency in Zurich before setting up on his own in 1963. He now works as art director and consultant for various advertising agencies. His works have appeared in international exhibitions in Tokyo, Warsaw, Toronto, and New York. In 1954, he won a prize offered by the City of Zurich, and in 1961 and 1971 two important prizes for posters in Italy. Geissbühler received awards in 1961 and 1963 in competition for Best Swiss Poster, and first prize at the 6th and 7th International Poster Biennale in Warsaw in 1976 and 1978. Geissbühler also obtained several first prizes in 1974 for emblems and packaging.

Ernst Hiestand

Ernst Hiestand received his education as a graphic designer at the Zurich Arts and Crafts School and as an apprentice. In 1960, with Ursula Hiestand he opened a studio for visual design, guide and information systems, corporate identity, packaging design, product design, industrial design, exhibition design, and photography. Since 1974, the Hiestands have been engaged in designing new bank notes and a new security system for the Swiss National Bank. Currently teaching at the Kunstgewerbeschule, Zurich, Ernst Hiestand has been guest lecturer at graphic design schools in Ulm, Offenbach, and Basel. Examples of the artists' work have been shown in many Swiss, European, and overseas exhibitions, and they have won over fifty national and international prizes. Since 1984, Ernst Hiestand has been design consultant for IBM Germany.

Dan Jonsson

Dan Jonsson received his professional training at Konstfackskolan in Stockholm from 1954 to 1958, and at the Kunstgewerbeschule in Basel in 1959. Before opening his own studio in 1965, he was art director at the Ervaco Agency, at Studio Martin Gawler, and at the Svea Agency. Since working freelance, he has been involved with graphic design and illustration in various fields. A one-man exhibition was held at Doktor Glas Gallery in Stockholm in 1969. He took part in the biennales in Venice in 1972, Brno in 1973 and 1979, and group exhibitions at the National Gallery in Stockholm in 1972 and 1980. He has received various awards, including the Artist Committee prize in 1971 and 1979, the Author Fund in 1972, the *Vi* illustrator prize in 1975, Stockholm's culture prize, and the Albert Bonnier 100 Years prize in 1976. Jonsson's works are represented in the collection of the National Gallery, Stockholm.

Georges Calame

Georges Calame set up his design studio in Geneva in 1953, collaborating from the outset with various international advertising agencies. Calame has specialized in exhibition design including the Italian pavilion at Graphic 57 (1956–1957), the communications and textile pavilions at the National Swiss Exhibition in 1964, "Man and the Sea" and the Belgian and Algerian pavilions at Expo '67, the Swiss pavilions at Brno in 1968 and the Milan Triennale (project, 1971), the Dybs 69 exhibition and publications, "Swiss Design" in Amsterdam (1970), and "Swiss Graphic Design" in Paris, Milan, Montreal, London, and Vienna (1970–1972). Calame was artistic director of the Pakistan Design Center (Karachi, 1969–1975). Designer of eleven Best Swiss Posters of the year from 1962 to 1982, Calame has designed the symbol/trademark for several international corporations. Involved in research into three-dimensionality, Calame designed the color graphics for the Geneva Central Post Office (1981).

Fritz Gottschalk

Fritz Gottschalk studied at the Kunstgewerbeschule in Zurich and Basel. After freelancing in Paris and working for industry in London, he moved to Canada in 1963. Gottschalk worked for Paul Arthur Associates on Expo '67 and then opened his own studio with Stuart Ash in 1966. Gottschalk + Ash International have won many awards for their work in the field of graphic design, corporate identity programs, systems design, industrial design, and architectural graphics. The team exhibited work at the Montreal Museum of Fine Arts in 1968, and in 1975 at Container Corporation of America in Chicago. In 1975, Gottschalk was asked by the Olympic Committee to direct the design and quality-control office. He frequently gives lectures on design, has been on many design committees, and was one of the judges of Spectrum '76, the RCA art exhibition of the 1976 Olympics. In 1978, Gottschalk moved back to Switzerland and opened the Gottschalk + Ash International office.

Ursula Hiestand

Ursula Hiestand trained in graphic art in Switzerland and in Paris. In 1960, a joint studio was opened with Ernst Hiestand in Zurich, and then later on in Zollikon. Since 1981, Ursula Hiestand heads the studio in Zollikon independently and under her own name, employing a team of assistants who work on group projects and occasionally with outside specialists. The studio, which serves mainly commercial and industrial clients, produces advertisements for the fashion industry, department stores, and shopping centers, cultural and commercial posters, packaging for foodstuffs, cosmetics, and technical products, trademarks, flyers, and interior and exterior decoration of buildings. For some years, she and Ernst Hiestand had been involved in the design of new bank notes and a new security system for the Swiss National Bank. Posters of Ursula Hiestand are in the Neue Sammlung, Staatliches Museum für angewandte Kunst, Munich.

Armin Hofmann
Armin Hofmann studied in Winterthur and in Zurich before going to work for several graphic design firms. He established his own studio in 1947, and in that same year secured a teaching position at the Basel School of Design. He has continued to pursue these complementary careers as designer and teacher ever since. Although principally based in Switzerland, he has long had a close relationship with the United States. In 1955, he was invited to lecture at Philadelphia College of Art, and the following year a similar offer was extended by Yale University. Since then he has continued on the faculties of both the Basel School of Design and Yale, while accepting numerous guest lectureships and speaking engagements at universities, schools of design, and professional design organizations. Hofmann's *Graphic Design Manual: Principles and Practice* was published in 1966. Recently he has collaborated closely with architects and planners, devoting considerable attention to projects exploring the use of color and graphic design in public places.

Peter Megert
Graphic designer Peter Megert was educated at the School of Applied Arts in Berne, and did post-graduate work at the University of Pittsburgh and Ohio State University. Megert's design work includes visual identity programs, printed materials, packaging, product graphics, exhibitions, architectural and environmental graphics, and multi-image presentations. Among honors awarded Megert's work have been national scholarships for outstanding performance in graphic design, citations for Best Swiss Poster of the year, and in 1982 a grant from the Ohio Arts Council. Megert has worked as graphic design consultant at the Westinghouse Corporate Design Center in Pittsburgh and has operated his own consulting and design practice, first in Berne and later in Columbus, Ohio. In 1985, Peter Megert and Michael Burke formed Visual Syntax Design with offices in Columbus and London. Megert is currently Professor of Design at Ohio State University, Columbus.

Josef Müller-Brockmann
Josef Müller-Brockmann studied widely before being apprenticed to a graphic designer in Zurich where he set up his own studio in 1936, specializing in exhibition design, commercial art, and photography. A contributor to the Swiss National Exhibition in Zurich in 1939, from 1942 to 1958 Müller-Brockmann designed stage sets for theaters in Zurich, Copenhagen, and Munich. Müller-Brockmann made the marionettes for the production of Hindemith's *Hin und Zurück* staged in Zurich in 1953. He has lectured at the International Design Conference in Aspen (1956), and at the World Design Conference in Tokyo (1960). In 1963, he lectured at the Hochschule für Gestaltung, Ulm, following a three-year teaching term at the Zurich Kunstgewerbeschule. Since 1966, Müller-Brockmann has been European design consultant for IBM. He lectured at Osaka Art University in 1970 and at Carleton University, Ottawa, in 1972. He has had one-man shows in Europe, Japan, and the United States.

Roger Pfund
Roger Pfund served an apprenticeship with Kurt Wirth in Berne, studying there at the Kunstgewerbeschule from 1963 to 1966. In 1966, 1967, and 1968, he was granted three federal scholarships for applied art. From 1969 to 1976, he was in partnership with Elisabeth Pfund. In 1969, he designed an exhibition for the centenary of the Schweizerische Volksbank. Pfund won first prize in a bank notes contest sponsored by the Swiss National Bank in 1971. Since 1976, he has been in partnership with Jean-Pierre Blanchoud. He has worked on the scheme of decoration for the military barracks in Wangen an der Aare and designed a 30-meter-long mural for the Schweizerische Volksbank in Neuchâtel. He specializes in bank notes, as well as computer graphics, figuring in an IBM film on this new art form. He is also involved in the design of cultural posters and books. Pfund designed the jubilee volume *75 Years of the Swiss National Bank*. In 1976, he won the Alice Bailly prize.

Ruedi Külling
Ruedi Külling studied at the Kunstgewerbeschule in Zurich. After working in 1956 as graphic artist with Franco Grignani in Milan, he joined Victor N. Cohen. In 1961, he went to Mather & Crowther in London, and from 1963 to 1966, he was art director at Advico-Delpire in Gockhausen, Zurich, becoming a manager in 1965. Külling spent one year in a similar post with Leo Burnett in Chicago, returning to Advico as creative director in charge of accounts in 1967. Since 1976, he has been a partner in Advico. He is also involved with SAWI, Biel (Swiss Training Center for Advertising and Information) as lecturer on creativity. Külling has received eight certificates of honor for best posters from the Swiss Federal Department of the Interior. He won a first prize in the Premio Rizzoli Pubblicità in 1963, a first prize for television commercial at the International Advertising Film Festival in Cannes, and a first prize for the Cementit ad from International Advertising Association.

Gérard Miedinger
After studies in Zurich and Paris, Gérard Miedinger worked as a freelance graphic designer for industrial firms, creating trademarks, logotypes, labels, lettering on buildings, and information brochures for public and commercial institutions. As exhibition designer, he was engaged for the Swiss pavilions in Brussels in 1958 and Montreal in 1967, and for international fairs of industry and commerce. He is well known for his window display for the Crédit Suisse, Zurich, for which he has been responsible since 1950. Miedinger specializes in the development of signage systems and corporate identity programs. He also organizes artistic contributions to architectural environments. In this capacity he served as art consultant and designer of interior decoration for the Crédit Suisse office building "Uetlihof" (1977–1981). Miedinger served as president of the Verband Schweizerischer Grafiker from 1968 to 1972.

Siegfried Odermatt
Siegfried Odermatt is self-taught. After working for a short period with an industrial graphic designer, he collaborated for three years on a freelance basis with Hans Falk. After an additional three years with an advertising agency, Odermatt opened his own studio in 1950. He was joined by Rosmarie Tissi in 1968. Recipient of awards at Typomundus in 1965 and 1970, Warsaw in 1970 and 1980, and Lahti in 1981, 1983, and 1985, Odermatt has together with his partner exhibited in New York, Stuttgart, Wuppertal, Hof-Saale, and Offenbach am Main.

Celestino Piatti
Celestino Piatti was trained at the Kunstgewerbeschule in Zurich. After an apprenticeship with Fritz Bühler in Basel, Piatti opened his own studio in 1948. Within a few years he produced a large volume of work comprising advertising campaigns, exhibition designs, illustration, packaging, and posters. In 1961, the Deutsche Taschenbuch Verlag entrusted him with the complete design of its paperbacks and relevant publicity. Since then Piatti has designed over three thousand book covers, utilizing empty space and white background as an integral graphic design element. Since 1968, Piatti has been increasingly involved in creating posters and art work for humanitarian projects. A first large retrospective of his work was shown at the Staatliche Museum, Kunstbibliothek, Berlin, in 1964. Piatti has received an award in the United States for his films *The Happy Owl* and *The Golden Feather of Plakanda*.

Edgar Reinhard
Edgar Reinhard received his professional training as a lithographer. He started his design career in advertising, subsequently specializing in three-dimensional design. Reinhard opened his own studio in 1971. His clients include multinational corporations such as IBM, and leading Swiss companies. Reinhard teaches at Ohio State University and at the summer workshop of Kent State University.

Rosmarie Tissi
Rosmarie Tissi studied at the School of Applied Arts in Zurich, then entered a four-year apprenticeship as a graphic designer. Since 1968, Tissi has been in partnership with Siegfried Odermatt. Three-time winner of Swiss scholarships for the applied arts, Tissi has received awards from Typomundus in 1965 and 1970, the Type Directors' Club of New York in 1966 and 1985, the 4th International Calendar Competition in Germany in 1972, the Warsaw Poster Biennale in 1970 and 1980, and at Lahti in 1981, 1983, and 1985. She has exhibited together with her partner in Stuttgart, Wuppertal, Hof-Saale, Offenbach am Main, and New York.

Kurt Wirth
Kurt Wirth was apprenticed in a graphic art studio from 1933 to 1936. He set up his own studio in 1937 doing illustrations for books and periodicals. Wirth has designed posters for Swissair, for exhibitions, and for tourist advertising. From 1952 to 1967, he designed more than one hundred eighty paperbacks and hardcover books, some illustrated, for Fischer Verlag, Frankfort, and for the pharmaceutical industry. He has had one-man shows in Berne, Zurich, Frankfort, and London between 1959 and 1966. Wirth has contributed to international exhibitions in Los Angeles, Toronto, Amsterdam, Hamburg, Honolulu, Milan, and New York. Since 1971, he has taught at the Kunstgewerbeschule in Berne. His book *Drawing, a Creative Process* won a gold medal and first prize at the International Biennale for Best Art Books in Israel in 1977.

Walter Allner
Walter Allner received his art training at the Bauhaus-Dessau under Albers, Kandinsky, Klee, and Schmidt. After settling in Paris, he became assistant to poster artist Jean Carlu and, later, partner in the design firm Omnium Graphique and art director for *Formes*. His paintings were shown at the Salon des Surindépendants and at the Salon des Réalités Nouvelles. Paris editor of *Graphis* from 1945 to 1948, he founded and edited the *International Poster Annual* in 1948, and was co-director of Editions Parallèles. In 1949, Allner went to the United States and did design and consultant work for many major companies. His work was part of the Fifty Years Bauhaus exhibition, which toured major museums around the world between 1968 and 1970. Since 1974, Allner has been teaching communication design at the Parsons School of Design in New York City. He is visiting critic at the Yale University School of Art. In 1979, he was recipient of the Bauhaus-Dessau medal of the German (Democratic Republic) Academy of Architecture.

Ruedi Rüegg
Ruedi Rüegg attended the Kunstgewerbeschule in Zurich. From 1960 to 1963, he served as graphic designer with J. Müller-Brockmann. He was assistant to Paul Rand in Connecticut, and from 1964 to 1965 he worked at the Nakamoto International Agency in Osaka, Japan, returning to Müller-Brockmann in 1965. From 1967 to 1976, he was co-owner of the agency MB & Co. in Zurich and in 1977 founded the agency Baltis and Rüegg in Zurich. Since 1968, he has been teaching as visiting professor at Ohio State University in Columbus. In 1976/1977, Rüegg was guest lecturer at the ETH in Zurich, and in 1981, at the Cooper Union School in New York. From 1973 to 1980, he was a member of the poster jury of the Federal Department of the Interior, and from 1976 to 1981, president of AGI Switzerland. Rüegg took part in group shows in Zurich in 1973, in Amsterdam in 1974, and in Milan in 1975. He has received several awards from the Swiss poster jury and the Poster Biennale in Warsaw.

Wolfgang Weingart
Wolfgang Weingart was trained as a lead-typesetter. Since 1968, he has taught typography at the Basel School of Design in Switzerland. For the past several years, he has also conducted typography workshops at the Yale University Summer Program in Graphic Design in Brissago, Switzerland. His teaching has focused on conventional and photographic experiments with typography. Since 1972, Weingart has lectured on his teaching methodologies in Switzerland, West Germany, Holland, Great Britain, and in the United States at the Cooper-Hewitt Museum, the California Institute of the Arts, Yale University, and Princeton University. Weingart is a contributor to the *Typographic Monatsblaetter,* St. Gall, and is founder of the periodicals *TM/Communication* and *Typographic Process*. His work has appeared in international design books and journals, and he has received awards from the Swiss Department of Cultural Affairs for his posters and book-cover designs.

Mark Zeugin
Mark Zeugin studied at the Design School in Luzern from 1948 to 1952, while working at a graphic design studio. He went to Schmidlin & Magoni, Basel, in 1953, and from 1954 to 1957 was art director with Werner Klapproth advertising agency. Since 1958, he has had his own graphic design studio in Luzern. Since 1965, the studio has been transformed into a design advertising agency. Zeugin was president of Bundes Grafischer Gestalter der Schweiz from 1963 to 1972, and president of Arbeitsgemeinschaft Schweizer Grafiker from 1972 to 1975. He teaches at the Design School, Biel.

Samuel N. Antupit
Samuel N. Antupit graduated from the Yale School of Art and Architecture in 1956. From 1958 to 1960, he was assistant art director at *Harper's Bazaar,* and from 1960 to 1962 at *Show* magazine. In 1962, he worked at Condé Nast Publications as assistant corporate art director, where he designed features for *Vogue, Mademoiselle, Glamour, House & Garden,* and special projects. Antupit was a member of Push Pin Studios (1963–1964), where he designed *The New York Review of Books* and *Art in America.* From 1964 to 1968, he was art director of *Esquire* magazine. From 1968 to 1978, Antupit ran his own company, Antupit & Others Inc., designers and consultants for book and magazine publishers, record companies, and corporate publications. His art direction of *Free to Be You and Me* won him an Emmy award. From 1978 to 1981, Antupit was executive art director for Book-of-the-Month Club, and since 1981 has been vice-president of art and design at Harry N. Abrams, Inc., publishers of fine illustrated books.

Saul Bass

Saul Bass studied at the Art Students' League with H. Trafton from 1936 to 1939 and at Brooklyn College with C. Kepes from 1944 to 1945. Bass was a freelance designer and art director in New York until moving to Los Angeles and founding Saul Bass Associates in 1946. Bass has directed short films and designed motion-picture titles and special sequences for films including *Psycho, Spartacus, Grand Prix,* the live-action epilogue for *West Side Story,* and the animated epilogue for *Around the World in 80 Days.* He has also designed for *Man with the Golden Arm, Anatomy of a Murder, Exodus, Such Good Friends,* and *That's Entertainment II.* Bass has designed numerous corporate identification systems for companies including the Bell System, United Airlines, Alcoa, and Rockwell International. He has had numerous one-man shows and group exhibitions in the United States and abroad. In 1969, Bass received an Oscar and a gold medal at the Moscow Film Festival for the documentary short *Why Man Creates.* He was named Art Director of the Year in 1957, and was elected to the New York Art Directors' Hall of Fame in 1978.

Ephram Edward Benguiat

Ephram Edward Benguiat studied at Columbia University and attended the Workshop School of Advertising Art in New York City. Contemplating a career in letter-form design, he worked as a designer and art director with many of the major advertising agencies and publishing companies in New York. Benguiat is vice-president and creative director at Photo-Lettering, Inc., and teaches at the School of Visual Arts and Columbia University. Vice-president of International Typeface Corporation, Benguiat is known for the more than five hundred typeface designs he has created. There are presently some ninety-two alphabets in the ITC collection designed by Benguiat, all of these mainstays of typographic usage worldwide.

R. O. Blechman

R. O. Blechman began his career as an illustrator immediately after graduating from Oberlin College in 1952. His first book of text and illustrations, *The Juggler of Our Lady,* was published the same year. He has worked for major magazines including *The New Yorker, Time,* and *Fortune,* and companies including IBM, Westinghouse, and Xerox. His drawings have been acknowledged with gold medals from art directors' clubs throughout the country, and with gallery shows in New York, Paris, Munich, and Berlin. Blechman's animated films have appeared in major international film festivals. In 1978, he produced *Simple Gifts,* a one-hour animated Christmas special for the Public Broadcasting System. His animated version of Igor Stravinsky's *L'Histoire du Soldat* was recently shown in Exxon's Great Performances series on PBS. Blechman is currently director of an animation studio in New York, The Ink Tank.

Peter Bradford

Peter Bradford worked for I. M. Pei, Time, and CBS before opening his own design and consulting firm in 1964. He has produced full design programs for many corporations and institutions such as CBS/Fawcett, Hitachi of Japan, National Educational Television, United States Information Agency, and the Ford Foundation. He was the creative director of a complete elementary reading textbook for Xerox Corporation's Ginn and Company. These projects, together with his magazine formats, books, documentary films, and illustrations, have won more than two hundred and fifty design show awards. He is represented in the permanent collections of the Library of Congress and the Cooper-Hewitt Museum. In 1978, he published *Chair,* his first independent book venture. He has juried many design shows, taught conceptual design for over fifteen years at the Philadelphia College of Art, the School of Visual Arts, and Cooper Union, is an advisor to the Silver Mountain Foundation, and a director of Documents of American Design.

Herbert Bayer

Herbert Bayer apprenticed in design studios following World War I. He studied mural painting under Kandinsky at the Bauhaus, Weimar (1921–1923), and from 1925 to 1928 taught typography and graphic design at the Bauhaus, Dessau. From 1928 to 1938, Bayer was active as a painter, photographer, graphic designer, and exhibition architect in Berlin. In 1938, he went to New York where he worked as an exhibition designer and a design consultant for government agencies and corporations. In 1946, Bayer was chosen as consultant for the development of Aspen, Colorado. Design consultant at Container Corporation of America (1946–1956), he was chairman of the design department from 1956 to 1965, and art director of their "Great Ideas of Modern Man" series. After 1966, Bayer worked as art and design consultant for Atlantic Richfield. His work includes painting and sculpture, graphic design, photography and photomontage, exhibition architecture, and environmental design and architecture.

Bruce Blackburn

Since 1973, Bruce Blackburn has been a principal in the New York design firm of Danne & Blackburn, Inc. Prior to that he was a partner in Chermayeff & Geismar Associates, during which time he designed the official U.S. Bicentennial symbol. Blackburn has served as consultant to NASA, the U.S. Department of Transportation, Champion International, IBM, Squibb, Mead, Dow Jones, Mobil, and the U.S. Army Corps of Engineers. He has served as Carnegie Professor of Graphic Design at Cooper Union in New York and visiting professor and lecturer at the University of Cincinnati, Philadelphia College of Art, Kent State University, and the Art Academy of Cincinnati. He is the author of *Design Standards Manuals,* a book published by the National Endowment for the Arts. Blackburn received the Presidential Award for Federal Design Excellence for his work on the National Aeronautics and Space Administration visual communications program.

Wilburn Bonnell

Wilburn Bonnell, a graduate of the University of Illinois in industrial design, joined Container Corporation of America in 1971, becoming manager of design in 1974. In 1978, he joined JC Penney in New York as manager of design development in packaging. In 1979, he formed his own design consulting office in New York. Bonnell has been involved with the Federal Design Improvement program as a panelist on design management and for design evaluation of government agencies. He designed and coordinated all the graphics for the Fourth Federal Design Assembly and was director of the Ryder Gallery in Chicago. He has taught at the Institute of Design and the Philadelphia College of Art. Bonnell has received over two hundred awards including the Art Directors' Club gold medal. His posters are in the permanent collection of the Museum of Modern Art in New York.

Cipe Pineles Burtin

Cipe Pineles Burtin started her career in the field of publication design at Condé Nast Publications, where her assignments included a year as art director of British *Vogue.* She became art director of *Seventeen* magazine shortly after it was launched by Helen Valentine. She also worked as art director for *Street* and *Charm* and *Mademoiselle.* Pineles Burtin was designer and design consultant for five years at Lincoln Center for the Performing Arts. For the past twenty years, Pineles Burtin has been a faculty member of Parsons School of Design and Director of Publication Design at Parsons. She has served on the visiting committee of Howard University's Graduate School of Design and is currently a member of the board of the American Institute of Graphic Arts. In 1985, she received the award of Continuing Excellence in Publication Design from the Society of Publication Designers. Pineles Burtin was the first woman elected to the Art Directors' Club and is the only woman inducted into its Hall of Fame.

Jacqueline S. Casey
Jacqueline S. Casey has been a graphic designer at the Massachusetts Institute of Technology since 1955. Currently director of Design Services at MIT, Casey exhibited her work in graphic design at the Directions 1968 exhibition at the Philadelphia College of Art, the Chelsea School of Art, London, in 1978, the MIT Hayden Gallery Corridor in 1972 and 1979, and the London College of Printing in 1980. Her posters have been included in national and international exhibitions and publications. Examples of her work have been acquired for the permanent collections of the Museum of Modern Art, New York, the Cooper-Hewitt Museum, the United States Information Agency, and the Library of Congress.

Seymour Chwast
Seymour Chwast studied at the Cooper Union School in New York before founding Push Pin Studios in 1954. In 1982, he founded a new firm, Pushpin Lubalin Peckolick, now the Pushpin Group, with Alan Peckolick. Chwast's designs and illustrations are used in advertising, animation, corporate and environmental graphics, record covers, books, magazines, posters, and packaging. He has created a variety of typefaces and designed and illustrated over a dozen children's books. Former publisher and art director of *Push Pin Graphic* and *Audience* magazines, Chwast founded the Push Pin Press. He has created background images for productions of *Candide* and the *Magic Flute*. Chwast is a recipient of the Saint-Gaudens medal and is a member of the Art Directors' Hall of Fame. His works are in the permanent collections of the Museum of Modern Art, the Cooper-Hewitt Museum, the Library of Congress, and the Gutenberg Museum. Chwast teaches at the Cooper Union School.

Richard Danne
Richard Danne has been an independent design consultant in Los Angeles and Dallas and, since 1963, in New York. Danne has served on numerous design juries and often lectures at design conferences and seminars. He has taught for many years at the School of Visual Arts, and has been visiting lecturer at other colleges and universities. Danne is involved in the development of both two- and three-dimensional design for many corporations and institutions in the United States. Recipient of major national and international design awards, Danne has received the Presidential Award for Design Excellence. Danne served two terms as president of the American Institute of Graphic Arts, and later served as founding president of AIGA/New York.

Paul Davis
Paul Davis attended the School of Visual Arts in New York and was a member of Push Pin Studios in its early days, before becoming an illustrator and graphic designer. His posters, particularly those for Joseph Papp's New York Shakespeare Festival, and his paintings have received international attention. *Paul Davis: Faces*, published by Friendly Press, is a collection of seventy full-color portraits of famous people done between the 1960s and the 1980s. His seventy-foot mural *Arcadian Scenes* is the focal point of a highly acclaimed New York restaurant. In 1984, Davis moved his studio from Sag Harbor to Manhattan.

Ivan Chermayeff
Ivan Chermayeff studied at Harvard University and graduated with a BFA from Yale University. In 1957, he helped found Brownjohn, Chermayeff & Geismar, which became Chermayeff & Geismar Associates in 1960. In 1973, he formed Art Planning Consultants to help client organizations in the assembling of art collections and the commissioning of works of art for buildings, offices, and public spaces. Former president of the American Institute of Graphic Arts, he is on the board of directors of the International Design Conference, Aspen, and the Municipal Art Society of New York. Chermayeff has served as Andrew Carnegie Visiting Professor of Art at Cooper Union. Among numerous awards, he has received the medal of the American Institue of Architects, the gold medal of the Philadelphia College of Art (1971), a special award for his contributions to the visual environment of New York City in 1974, and the Claude M. Fuess award in 1979. In 1979, Chermayeff and Geismar received a gold medal from the American Institute of Graphic Arts.

James Cross
James Cross began his career as a corporate art director for the Rand Corporation and Northrop Corporation after graduating from UCLA's School of Fine Arts in 1956. He taught concurrently at UCLA until 1963, when he went to Saul Bass and Associates as designer. The same year he opened his own firm which now has offices in Los Angeles and San Francisco. From 1960 to 1966, he served on the board of directors of the International Design Conference in Aspen. Cross taught graphic design at the Art Center College of Design from 1970 to 1972, has served on the advisory board of the Art Center College of Design since 1978, and was a director of the American Institute of Graphic Arts from 1976 to 1979. Cross is a frequent lecuturer at universities and professional organizations and is a recipient of numerous design awards.

Louis Danziger
Louis Danziger began as an apprentice in the art department of a New York printing firm at the age of fifteen. In 1947, he studied at the Art Center School in Los Angeles under Alvin Lustig, and in 1948 at the New School under Alexey Brodovitch. Danziger worked as a freelance designer at *Esquire* (1949) until his return to California, where he has since worked as a freelance designer and consultant for clients including Dreyfus, Container Corporation of America, and Atlantic Richfield. Since 1947, Danziger has been design consultant to the Los Angeles County Museum of Art. A teacher at the Art Center School of Design from 1956 to 1962, and the Chouinard Art Institute from 1963 to 1972, he is currently head of the graphic design program at California Institute of the Arts. He has lectured on the history of graphic design at many universities. His work is represented in the collections of the Museum of Modern Art, New York, the Los Angeles County Museum of Art, and the Library of Congress.

Rudolph de Harak
Rudolph de Harak began his career as a designer in studios and agencies before opening his own design office in New York in 1950. Specializing in graphic and environmental and exhibition design, his work has been exhibited in major exhibitions in New York and Paris and was included in the U.S. Information Agency exhibition to the Soviet Union in 1963 and the Far East in 1964. In addition to his professional design practice, de Harak has been a teacher of design and visual communications since 1952. He is was a visiting professor at Yale University and professor of design at the Cooper Union School of Art and Architecture. De Harak was a member of the advisory committee to the United States Department of Transportation for the development of symbols for use in transportation related facilities. He has received awards from the American Institute of Architects, the American Institute of Graphic Arts, the New York Art Directors' Club, and the New York Type Directors' Club. In 1981, de Harak was recipient of a grant from the National Endowment for the Arts for research in the history of design.

195

Louis Dorfsman
Louis Dorfsman graduated from the Cooper Union School of Art and Architecture, which awarded him a Citation for Outstanding Professional Achievement in 1956, and in 1963 its highest alumni distinction, the Augustus Saint-Gaudens medal. Now Vice-President, Creative Director, Corporate Advertising and Design at CBS Inc., Dorfsman joined CBS as a staff designer in 1946. Past president of the New York Art Directors' Club, he has received from that organization thirteen gold medals and twenty-three awards of distinctive merit. In 1978, he was inducted into the Art Directors' Club Hall of Fame and received the American Institute of Graphic Arts gold medal. In 1979, Dorfsman won an Emmy award for television opening titles and two Clio awards for television commercials and advertisements. He is a member of the board of trustees of the Cooper Union School of Art and Architecture and the board of directors of the International Design Conference in Aspen, which he chaired in 1979.

Gene Federico
After graduating from Pratt Institute in 1938, Gene Federico worked for a small advertising agency in New York. This budding career was interrupted by service with the U.S. Army, where he continued to design murals and posters and organized an exhibition of soldiers' paintings in Oran. After the war, he worked successively for Grey Advertising, Doyle Dane Bernbach, Benton and Bowles, and Warwick and Legler, until 1967 when he helped found Lord, Geller, Federico, Einstein Inc. Federico creates advertising campaigns and corporate images in all media. His many awards include those of the New York Art Directors' Club, the American Institute of Graphic Arts, and the Type Directors' Club of New York. His work was shown in an exhibition of international graphic design in London in 1978. In November 1980, he was inducted into the Art Directors' Club Hall of Fame.

Thomas H. Geismar
Thomas H. Geismar concurrently attended Brown University and Rhode Island School of Design, and subsequently received a master's degree from Yale University. As a partner in Chermayeff & Geismar Associates, he has been responsible for the design of over one hundred corporate identification programs for companies such as Mobil, Xerox, Burlington, Chase Manhattan Bank, Best Products, Owens-Illinois, PBS, and Rockefeller Center. Geismar has developed major U.S. government exhibitions at the international expositions in Montreal, New York, and Osaka. Currently involved with exhibit planning for the restored Statue of Liberty and Ellis Island, Geismar has also guided development of a new national system of standardized symbols. In 1985, he received one of the first Presidential Design Awards for this effort. Along with partner Chermayeff, he received the gold medal from the American Institute of Graphic Arts in 1979, and in 1983 the First International Design Award from the Japan Design Foundation.

Milton Glaser
Milton Glaser studied at Cooper Union in New York, obtaining a Fulbright scholarship to continue his studies at the Accademia di Belle Arti in Bologna. In 1954, he was instrumental in founding Push Pin Studios. In 1968, Glaser became design director and chairman of the board of *New York* magazine, and in 1975 vice-president and design director of the *Village Voice*. Since 1974, he has been president of Milton Glaser Inc. Glaser is currently involved in producing graphic design, signage, theming, packaging, and corporate identity programs. Recipient of a gold medal from the American Institute of Graphic Arts and the Saint-Gaudens medal of the Cooper Union School, Glaser was co-chairman of the International Design Conference in Aspen in 1973, and in 1979 became an honorary fellow of the Royal Society of Arts. Glaser is represented in the collections of the Museum of Modern Art, New York, the Israel Museum, Jerusalem, the Victoria and Albert Museum, and the Musée de l'Affiche, Paris.

Charles and Ray Eames
Charles Eames studied architecture at Washington University and practiced architecture in St. Louis from 1924 to 1936. Eames studied with Eliel Saarinen and taught design at Cranbrook Academy of Art, Bloomfield Hills, Michigan, from 1936 to 1941. Charles Eames died in 1978.

Ray Kaiser Eames studied painting with Hans Hofmann from 1933 to 1939, and went to Cranbrook in 1940. Married in 1941, the Eameses designed furniture, toys, exhibitions, architecture, and motion pictures.

Colin Forbes
Colin Forbes studied at the London Central School of Arts and Crafts. After a period as a freelance designer and lecturer at the Central School, he became an advertising agency art director. He was then appointed head of the graphic design department at the Central School. In 1960, Forbes established his own design practice, having been appointed design consultant to Pirelli in England, and soon afterwards joined with designers Alan Fletcher and Bob Gill to form the partnership Fletcher/Forbes/Gill. In the early 1970s, the development and expansion of the partnership resulted in the formation of Pentagram. Forbes is currently partner of Pentagram, New York, and in addition to his design activities he is also the group's executive partner internationally. From 1972 to 1975, he was a member of the British Design Council; in 1973, he was elected Royal Designer for Industry by the Royal Society of Arts. In 1977, Forbes was granted the President's Award of the Designers' and Art Directors' Association in London for his outstanding contribution to design.

Stephan Geissbuhler
Stephan Geissbuhler received a degree in graphic design from the School of Art and Design in Basel in 1964. He subsequently joined the design and promotion division of the J. R. Geigy Pharmaceutical Company in Basel. In 1967, he moved to the United States to teach graphic design at the Philadelphia College of Art. Concurrently from 1968 to 1971, Geissbuhler was associate designer with Murphy, Levy, Wurman in Philadelphia. In 1975, he joined Chermayeff & Geismar Associates in New York, and was made a partner in 1979. Geissbuhler has been in charge of graphics for major projects such as the bicentennial exhibit for the Smithsonian Institution, a traveling exhibit marking the American Chemical Society's centennial year, and an identity and communications system for the U.S. Environmental Protection Agency. Geissbuhler served on the board of the American Institute of Graphic Arts as vice-president and is currently president of the New York chapter. He is also a member of the faculty for the improvement of federal graphics.

Tomás Gonda
Tomás Gonda, educated in Hungary, began his career in Argentina in advertising agencies. In 1952, he opened his own office in Buenos Aires, designing graphics for Aerolineas Argentinas, gallery and museum publications, and the Argentinian pavilion at Expo 58 in Brussels. In 1958, Gonda was invited to the Hochschule für Gestaltung in Ulm where he taught until 1967. His work of this period includes design programs for Lufthansa, Braun, Wilkahn, and Herman Miller. In the 1970s in Milan, he became design director of Rinascente/Upim and later of Pirelli Industries. He opened his office in New York in 1979, designing for corporate clients including Booz, Allen & Hamilton Inc., IBM, Savin Corporation, Champion Papers, and Xerox. Gonda has taught at Ohio State University, Yale University, SUNY at Purchase, Cooper Union, Rhode Island School of Design, the University of Washington, and Carnegie Mellon University. Gonda's work is represented in numerous private collections.

April Greiman
April Greiman studied graphic design at the Kansas City Art Institute, and the Allgemeine Kunstgewerbeschule, Basel, with Wolfgang Weingart and Armin Hofmann. After working in New York and Philadelphia, she moved to California where she began, in 1976, to produce the work for which she is now well known. Greiman works in graphic design, packaging, interiors, and television production for clients including Inference Corporation, Xerox, Sasson, and Esprit.

Toshihiro Katayama
Toshihiro Katayama is self-taught as an artist. From 1952 to 1960, he worked as a freelance graphic designer in Osaka, subsequently co-founding Nippon Design Center. Katayama spent three years in Switzerland at the invitation of Geigy, Basel. In 1965, he joined the Persona group in Japan. Invited to the United States in 1966 by the Carpenter Center for Visual Arts, Harvard University, he is currently senior lecturer and designer at the Carpenter center. Katayama has designed more than twenty exhibitions, and in 1974 collaborated with Octavio Paz in presenting *Three Notations/Rotations.* In 1972, he designed ten banners for the Harvard Architecture Department. He has had more than fifteen shows of his work since 1965 in Switzerland, Japan, the United States, Canada, and Austria. Since 1975, he has designed signage and environmental graphics and sculpture, including murals for the Boston subway and a sculptural work for Tange's Akasaka Prince Hotel, Tokyo. Katamaya's work has been collected and published by the Museum of Modern Art, New York.

John Massey
John Massey studied advertising design at the University of Illinois and later served as art director for the university press. He joined the Container Corporation of America in 1957, was appointed advertising and design manager in 1961 and director of design, advertising, and public relations in 1964. He is currently devoting his time to his own design practice in Chicago. Massey's work gives priority to clear visual and verbal communication, while paintings and screen prints derive from a preoccupation with geometrical patterns and volumes. Massey served as instructor at the Illinois Institute of Technology and is currently advisor to the International Design Conference in Aspen, and other bodies. Massey was named Art Director of the Year by the National Society of Art Directors' in 1967, and was awarded a gold medal by the New York Art Directors' Club in 1979.

Arthur Paul
Arthur Paul is a freelance designer and consultant for magazines, advertising, television, and feature films. He is the founding art director of *Playboy* magazine, having designed the *Playboy* rabbit logo and the first issue of the magazine in 1953. After twenty-nine years as vice-president/art director at *Playboy*, he left to pursue a more diversified art and design career. Through the years he has won numerous awards and honors for his work. He is on the advisory board of the Society of Publication Designers in New York, and is a trustee of the Museum of Contemporary Art in Chicago. He recently became an honored alumnus of the Institute of Design, ITT, and an honorary member of the Artists' Guild of Chicago and is on the advisory board of the Association of Corporate Art Curators in Chicago.

Richard Hess
Richard Hess studied at Michigan State University, then joined Palmer Paint Company where he painted originals of the first paint-by-number sets. From 1955 to 1957, he was art director with J. Walter Thompson in Detroit. After one year with Grant Advertising, he moved to Philadelphia to work as art group director for print and television with N. W. Ayer. In 1962, he joined Benton and Bowles in New York and in 1965, after a year as creative director for Van Brunt Advertising, founded Richard Hess Inc. As graphic and film art consultant, Hess has numbered among his clients CBS, Pepsico, IBM, Xerox, Du Pont, and periodicals *Esquire, New York* magazine, and the *New York Times.* Since 1957, Hess has received almost annually the awards of the New York Art Directors' Club. Hess's work is represented in the collections of the Museum of Modern Art, New York, the National Portrait Gallery and Library of Congress, Washington, D.C., and the Amon Carter Museum, Fort Worth, Texas.

Leo Lionni
Leo Lionni is self-taught as a graphic artist. He did his first abstract paintings in 1925 and in the same year contributed to *Giornale di Genova.* He was invited by Marinetti in 1932 to join the Futurist movement and became active in Milanese art circles, doing paintings and graphics and writing reviews. After emigrating to the United States in 1939, he joined N. W. Ayer advertising agency, becoming one of the first to use free art for advertising and giving commissions to Moore, Léger, De Kooning, and others. In 1949, he became art director of *Fortune* and design director with Olivetti America. From 1962, he concentrated on writing and illustrating children's books, winning many international awards. Lionni moved to Italy in 1962, and in 1970 began work for *Imaginary Botanics.* Lionni received five major awards for animated films at the 1970 Tehran Film Festival. He was elected to the Art Directors' Hall of Fame in 1974.

Tomoko Miho
Tomoko Miho currently heads her own design office, Tomoko Miho Co., in New York. Noted for the highly refined sensibility of her work, Miho designed the posters for the Smithsonian National Air and Space Museum's Bicentennial celebration in 1976, and the banners and symbols for the United States pavilion at the 1982 Energy Expo. In her continued association with Herman Miller Inc., in 1984 Miho designed the display for West Week at the Herman Miller showroom in Los Angeles; she was also responsible for the concept and planning of the New York showroom's Designers' Saturday. Formerly head of graphics with George Nelson and Company in New York, and design manager for the Center for Advanced Research in Design, Miho is design consultant for Champion International Corporation. From 1979 to 1982, Miho was a member of the board of directors of the American Institute of Graphic Arts. Her posters are in the permanent collection of the Museum of Modern Art, New York.

Alan Peckolick
Alan Peckolick studied at Pratt Institute, and worked for McCann-Erickson and Kenyon & Eckhardt. In 1964, he joined Herb Lubalin as graphic designer and four years later opened his own studio. In 1973, he joined Lubalin, Smith, Carnase as vice-president and creative director and held the same positions in Herb Lubalin Associates from 1978 to 1980, when he became president of Lubalin, Peckolick Associates. Peckolick joined with Seymour Chwast in 1982 to form Pushpin Lubalin Peckolick, now the Pushpin Group. He has achieved international recognition for his elegantly designed and executed typefaces. The recipient of numerous awards, Peckolick is a frequent lecturer and juror. His work is represented in the permanent collection of the Gutenberg Museum.

Woody Pirtle
Woody Pirtle began his career in Dallas in 1969 with the Richards Group. He formed Pirtle Design in 1978, offering graphic consultation and creative services to major corporations, public relations firms, and advertising agencies. The firm functions as catalyst and coordinator on projects ranging from corporate identity programs and annual reports to packaging and point of purchase materials. Pirtle was named Individual Communicator of the Year by the Art Directors' Club of Houston in 1979 and 1981, and received both Individual and Corporate Communicator of the Year awards in 1982. Consistently represented in the major annual design competitions, Pirtle is editorial advisor to the Japanese magazine *Portfolio*. In 1983, Pirtle was one of the fourteen named by *Adweek* to the 1983 All American Creative Team. He was elected to the board of directors of the American Institute of Graphic Arts in 1982.

Arnold Saks
Arnold Saks graduated from Syracuse University and studied at the Yale School of Design. He set up his own design office in 1967, and works in the major areas of graphic design: annual reports, booklets, trademarks and corporate identity, publications, architectural graphics, and exhibition design. Among his firm's corporate clients are Alcoa, American Home Products, Avon, Bethlehem Steel, Bristol-Myers, Burlington Industries, Colt Industries, Goldman Sachs, Knoll Furniture, Marine Midland, Monsanto, Norton, Peat/Marwick, Pitney Bowes, RCA, SCM, Seagram, Sohio, Squibb, and United Technologies. Saks has been visiting lecturer at Cooper Union, the School of Visual Arts, and Parsons School of Design. His firm has an international reputation and has won major awards in the United States and Europe.

Louis Silverstein
Louis Silverstein, a design consultant, for many years was chief designer, corporate art director, and assistant managing editor of the *New York Times*. He has designed other newspapers and been design consultant for *Jornal do Brazil*, *Dagens Nyeter* of Stockholm, the *Times* of London, and the *International Herald Tribune*. Silverstein has designed numerous other publications, books, and corporate materials. His work was represented in the U.S. State Department's exhibit of U.S. graphics in Russia in 1963 and in a traveling show of posters in 1958. Silverstein is a painter and member of the American Abstract Artists, with whom he exhibits. He has taught at the School of Visual Arts, and lectured extensively in the United States and abroad. In 1984, he was awarded the Herb Lubalin Award for lifetime achievement from the Society of Publication Designers. The same year Silverstein won election into the Hall of Fame of the New York Art Directors' Club.

Bradbury Thompson
Bradbury Thompson studied at Washburn University. After working at Capper Publications, he became art director first with Rogers-Kellog-Stillson, then from 1942 to 1945 with the Office of War Information and from 1945 to 1959 with *Mademoiselle* magazine. From 1938 to 1962, he designed *Westvaco-Inspirations*, the house organ of Westvaco Corporation, and was consultant for *Art News* from 1945 to 1972. Since 1959, Bradbury has designed art books and magazines and has acted as consultant designer to leading publishers, universities, and corporations. Faculty member since 1956 at Yale University School of Art and Architecture and since 1968 a member of the board of trustees of Washburn University, Bradbury has had one-man exhibitions of his work in towns across the United States. He has received many awards including the National Society of Art Directors' gold T-Square in 1950 and the Pimny Power of Printing award in 1980. His work is represented in the collection of the Museum of Modern Art, New York.

Paul Rand
Paul Rand studied at Pratt Institute, Parsons School of Design, and the Art Students' League, under George Grosz, in New York. He was art director at *Esquire* and *Apparel Arts* from 1937 to 1941, and at the William H. Weintraub advertising agency from 1941 to 1954. Rand taught at Cooper Union, and from 1956 at the Yale University School of Art and Architecture. He is now Professor Emeritus at Yale. A consultant to leading firms, he is also distinguished for contribution to book design and illustration and has written books and articles describing the principles and disciplines governing his work. Rand was awarded an honorary professorship at Tama University, Tokyo, in 1958, a citation from the Philadelphia College of Art in 1962, and a gold medal from the American Institute of Graphic Arts in 1966. He was elected to the first New York Art Directors' Hall of Fame in 1972. Rand was granted an honorary Doctor of Fine Arts degree from the Philadelphia College of Art in 1979.

Arnold Schwartzman
Arnold Schwartzman began his career as a designer in television, and as an illustrator contributed regularly to the London *Sunday Times*. After a time in advertising, he became director of the Conran Design Group. In 1979, Schwartzman set up his own design studio, while continuing as the principal of the Designers Film Unit, and as a film director with Directors Studio, London. In 1978, Schwartzman moved to Los Angeles to become design director with Saul Bass & Associates. In 1982, he was appointed director of design to the Los Angeles Olympic Organizing Committee. Schwartzman co-authored *Airshipwreck* with Len Deighton, and is the author of *Flicks–The Magic of the Movies,* a multidimensional book on precinema history. A lecturer and external examiner to many art institutions in the United Kingdom and the United States, Schwartzman has received numerous design and film awards, including an Oscar for his documentary film *Genocide*.

Deborah Sussman
Deborah Sussman's career began in the office of Charles and Ray Eames (1953–1957, 1961–1967), designing graphics, showrooms, films, toys, and exhibits, including the Nehru Memorial Exhibit and IBM Pavilion at the New York World's Fair (1964). Winner of a Fulbright scholarship in graphics to the Hochschule für Gestaltung, Ulm, in 1957, Sussman worked with Danese and Studio Boggeri in Milan and Galeries Lafayette in Paris from 1958 to 1960. Sussman opened her own design office in 1968. Fulbright lecturer in India in 1976, Sussman has conducted an extensive photographic survey of street design in Europe, Mexico, and Asia. Married to Paul Prejza, Sussman incorporated Sussman/Prejza & Co. in 1980. A teacher at the University of Southern California, the Art Center College of Design, Cal Arts, and UCLA, Sussman's design work at the 1984 Los Angeles Olympics is her major work to date, pioneering in the integration of graphics and architecture in a new category of urban design.

Fred Troller
Fred Troller graduated from the Kunstgewerbeschule, Zurich, in 1950. In 1954, he worked for film producer Louis de Rochemont, traveling widely in North and Central America. He ran his own design studio in Zurich until 1960, then spent six years as art director with Geigy Chemical Corporation in the United States. Troller currently heads a design studio in Rye, New York, working on advertising and corporate design for a wide range of companies. Influenced by Swiss traditions of design but stimulated by the dynamic climate of New York, Troller views his own style as a synthesis of new visual images and techniques. Participant in exhibitions in the United States and abroad and in the American Institute of Graphic Arts traveling shows, Troller has won numerous certificates and awards of excellence from the American Institute of Graphic Arts and from the New York Art and Type Directors' Clubs.

George Tscherny
George Tscherny began his professional career as packaging designer with Donald Deskey & Associates in 1950. He joined George Nelson & Associates as graphic designer in 1953, and in 1955 opened his own design office. Tscherny is active in the field of corporate and institutional communications. His assignments have ranged from the design of a commemorative postage stamp for the U.S. Postal Service to identification programs for corporations such as W. R. Grace & Co. and Texasgulf. Other clients have included Air Canada, American Can Co., Burlington Industries, CPC International, General Dynamics, IBM, Johnson & Johnson, Mobil, Morgan Stanley, Pan American Airways, JC Penney, RCA, and Rockwell International. Tscherny has taught design at Pratt Institute and the School of Visual Arts, and lectured as Mellon Visiting Professor at Cooper Union. Several of Tscherny's poster designs are in the permanent collection of the Museum of Modern Art, New York.

Dietmar Winkler
Dietmar R. Winkler was educated in design at the Kunstschule Alsterdamm in Hamburg and the Rhode Island School of Design. Combining a professional design practice with the teaching of design and communication theory, he is currently tenured professor of design at Southeastern Massachusetts University. Winkler specializes in the development of complex design and typographic systems for the organization of abstract data. He has worked as type and design director for the Massachusetts Institute of Technology, WGBH Educational Foundation, and Southeastern Massachusetts University. He is design consultant to the Harvard Business School, Wellesley College, Brandeis University, the Educational Development Center, and Ginn & Company. Winkler's work has been exhibited by major professional organizations including the art directors' clubs of Boston, New York, and St. Louis, the Type Directors' Club of New York, and the American Institute of Graphic Arts.

Massimo Vignelli
Massimo Vignelli studied at Accademia di belli arti, Milan, and the School of Architecture of the University of Venice. He has been a member of the Italian Association for Industrial Design since its founding in 1956 and served on the board of directors from 1960 to 1964. Between 1958 and 1964, he taught at the Institute of Design of Illinois Institute of Technology in Chicago, at the Umanitaria School of Graphic Design in Milan, and at the Institute of Industrial Design in Venice. In 1960, he established with Elena Vignelli an office of design and architecture in Milan, working as visual, product, furniture, and exhibition designer and consultant for major European companies and institutions. From 1965 to 1971, he established an office in New York. In 1985, Vignelli was recipient of the Presidential Design Award for the comprehensive graphics program which he designed for the National Park Service.

Henry Wolf
Henry Wolf started working as a designer in 1946, becoming art director of *Esquire* magazine in 1952, *Harper's Bazaar* in 1958, and *Show* magazine in 1961. In 1964, he joined Jack Tinker and Partners as a creative partner, two years later becoming art director of the Center of Advanced Practice at McCann-Erickson. In 1966, he became partner/creative director at Trahey Wolf Advertising. In 1971, Wolf started his own design and photography studio, with diverse clients ranging from IBM and GTE to Saks Fifth Avenue, Herman Miller, and Champion Paper. Henry Wolf is a member of the Hall of Fame of the Art Directors' club, recipient of the American Institute of Graphic Arts gold medal in 1976, a Benjamin Franklin Fellow of the Royal Society of the Arts, London, director of the Aspen Design Conference, and winner of numerous medals and awards. He teaches at Parsons School of Design, and has taught at the School of Visual Arts and Cooper Union since 1957.

Index